The Talk and Beyond

RAISING YOUR CHILDREN
IN
A CONFUSED CULTURE

Michael Moynihan

Scepter

Previous books by Michael Moynihan, published by Scepter:

*The Father and His Family: A Guidebook for Aspiring,
New, and Experienced Fathers*

*Decisive Parenting: Forming Authentic Freedom
in Your Children*

Published by Scepter Publishers, Inc.
info@scepterpublishers.org
www.scepterpublishers.org
800-322-8773
New York

All rights reserved.
Cover design by Marc Whitaker, MTWdesign
Text design and composition by Rose Design

Library of Congress Control Number: 2021949370
ISBN paperback: 9781594174469
ISBN eBook: 9781594174476

Printed in the United States of America

Contents

Introduction

I pull our van into the driveway, returning from a family trip. We are about to unload. I begin the familiar challenge of organizing our children's efforts to help put things in their proper places.

"Dad, I need to talk to you."

I turn and see one of my older sons and am just about to tell him to wait until we unpack, when I see a look in his eye that gives me pause. He notices my hesitation. "It is important. I need to ask you something."

A knowing look passes between my wife and me. She takes over and I walk a few steps away into our garage with my son. "Yes, son. What is it?"

"Dad, when we talked before about growing up from a boy to a man, you mentioned to me that I can come to you at any time if I have a question or if something comes up."

As I listened, an overwhelming sense of gratitude and relief came over me. As with most matters related to the maturing of a young heart and the accompanying physical and emotional changes that take place, the matter was easily cleared up with a few words of fatherly perspective. But this conversation would never have come up if I had not first approached my son earlier and talked with him about God's plan for human love and the changes that hearts and bodies go through as we grow up. I purposely did not give him too much information the first time we talked. Respecting his innocence, I stuck to the theme of the goodness of God's plan for men, women, and marital love. I mentioned that while these growing-up changes might be confusing, it is always okay to ask me about any questions or concerns that arise.

This conversation I had with my son represents the imperative need for healthy communication between parents and their children. Fathers have just as much wisdom to impart to their daughters as to their sons, just as mothers have invaluable insight for their sons just as they do for their daughters.

Many parents are uncertain and anxious about how to help their children grow into mature and responsible adults. They want their children to embrace God's plan for marital love. Seeing the confusion about the definition of marriage, they fear children turning away from God's plan. Parents can wonder how they should help navigate this subject. How should they teach their children, and talk to them?

......

This book attempts to provide thoughtful parents with practical guidance on how to help their children understand and live God's plan for the human heart, with all its attractions and possibilities. Though this book is written with an eye to the challenges we face in today's culture, much of what is said would apply to all times and places since these matters are rooted in human nature. This book builds on some of the key points made in my first book, *The Father and His Family*:

- Fathers should tell their sons about God's plan for the love between a man and a woman before they hear a reductive version of this topic elsewhere: the same applies for mothers and daughters.
- When talking to their child about the love between a man and a woman, it is not necessary for parents to get into the mechanics too early. The term "marital embrace" is often enough.

- It is helpful for parents to mention that the changes that take place in the heart and the body are fundamentally good and part of God's plan, and that these changes speak to the call to marriage for the majority of people.

- Parents should alert their children to the inner weakness of our fallen nature and the battle that the devil is waging against pure love in our society, giving concrete pointers on how to respond when they face attractions within and are presented with problematic content and situations.

Raising a child to love with a pure heart is no small task, especially when faced with a culture that makes it difficult for some to even know what it means to talk about true love. St. Josemaría Escrivá used to talk about the human heart as made for love. He noted that we love God with the same heart with which we love others.[1] He asserted that a popular love song or ballad, intended to describe the love between a man and a woman, could also be addressed to God as a prayer. This approach is hardly unique:

---

1. Josemaría Escrivá, *Friends of God* (New York: Scepter, 2002), 229.

The Song of Songs from the Old Testament draws strong parallels between human and divine love.

But how much of the contemporary popular understanding of human love is still open to this interpretation? Popular art, including literature, films, and music, do not display the same discretion as was typical sixty years ago. Although people still write popular love songs that can be interpreted as referring to committed marital love—and I would argue that any wholesome song that reflects spousal love between a man and a woman could also by analogy refer to Christ's love for his Church—there are also popular songs that reference a baser side of human attraction. Lust and love are not the same thing.

This book is written for busy parents. It presents practical points on guiding children of various ages, including what messages parents should communicate to their children and when to communicate them. It also has guidance for some common challenges that can arise. We are complicated creatures and things do not always proceed smoothly. And the times we live in arguably make this more difficult in certain ways than in previous times. Without as many wholesome cultural examples of authentic masculinity and femininity, parents can find a great source of assistance from well-chosen literature. There are several suggestions for works of literature, both classics and some more recent works, that illustrate deep truths about human love, and help to form the moral imagination. A final section of the book focuses on living the virtue of holy purity and is full of practical guidance that can be passed on to children at the right time.

This book is, of course, informed both by my personal efforts to reflect on my own experience and by a fair amount of study. Working at an all-boys school with a distinct mission to help parents with the integral formation of their sons, I am privileged to observe many families. These life lessons and observations, of course, do not just apply to our sons, but to our daughters as well. Throughout my professional life I have striven to acquire a liberal arts education and to study contemporary challenges in a way that is informed by the wisdom of the past. In doing so, I have keenly come to realize parenting mistakes I have made, many small ones and a few larger ones. So as you read this, keep in mind that some of what follows is not what I actually did, but what I now realize is what I should have done.

The perfect family does not exist. All have complications and experience suffering, some of their own making. This is certainly the case with our family. Even so, my wife and I are convinced that what children most need is not perfect parents who do everything right, but rather parents who keep striving and who know how to apologize when necessary. In fact, if we present ourselves as perfect, knowing full well we aren't, we are not giving our children the environment they need to learn through their mistakes as they grow in virtue.

As we focus on boys and girls growing into integrated men and women, we will necessarily need to maintain a broad perspective. We love as human persons, as men and women with hearts made to form attachments to what is good. Ultimately these hearts are ennobled and fulfilled by loving the greatest good, God himself. But we are made to live in history. And so the restlessness of our hearts directs us as we seek various goods in the context of a complete life, with numerous material details and events that bring both joys and sorrows.

CHAPTER 1

The Fundamentals

The normal and by far most common way for a baby to be conceived and born is either male or female.[1] More than just a biological fact, clear from indisputable anatomical differences, this embodiment as either male or female is integral to the way each person has been created. Near the beginning of his pontificate, St. John Paul II devoted several Wednesday audiences to reflecting on the anthropological implications of the first chapters of Genesis, including the passage "God created man in his own image, in the image of God he created him; male and female he created them" (Gn 1:27). We are in the image of God

---

1. A small number of persons are born with both male and female traits, a situation usually caused by a hormonal condition, although some are genetically born neither simply male nor simply female. These persons are of course not outside God's plan. God wants them to reach the heights of holiness, as is his will for every person. In some cases, intersex persons can get medical help to develop as either a man or a woman. And even when such a condition is a source of suffering it is nonetheless the case that all suffering, including a condition one is born with, has the possibility of being meaningfully transformed through union with God.

both as individual human persons and as created male and female, with the possibility of living in communion with each other. St. John Paul II explores both of these dimensions through reflecting on what he calls "original solitude" and "original unity."[2]

The human person is in the image of God as a "solitary" individual person with a rational nature, an intellect and a will, that sets him or her above the rest of material creation. The various animals were interesting to the first man, who worked at "naming" them, but none of them were akin to him and capable of satisfying his longing for friendship, for communion with one like himself. He experienced his place among material creation as an "original solitude."The recognition of his unique place in creation led to a longing for transcendence, for knowledge and love. The longings of the human heart speak to the fact that we are made to be in relation to other persons, that we are incomplete as solitary individuals. This orientation toward relation is reflected in our bodies, each person created male or female. One's identity as a man or woman includes relationality woven into our nature, an inner

2. John Paul II, General Audiences (November 7, 1979; November 14, 1979). Vatican website: *www.vatican.va.*

directedness toward other persons and in a special way to the opposite sex. St. John Paul II sees this relational aspect of our humanity as directed toward a *communio personarum* or "communion of persons," as able to lead to a unity that is also indicative of being created in the image of God. "Original unity" replaces and transcends "original solitude" through the communion of persons. Just as God is a Trinity of Persons—Father, Son and Holy Spirit—so the love between a man and a woman can be fruitful in an analogous way.

That we are embodied persons in this way, as men and women, is both significant and a great good. Masculinity and femininity are complementary and oriented toward each other.[3] The love between a man and a woman finds its essential meaning and expression in committed marital love that is open to new life, to the forming of a family as a *communio personarum*. In such a family authentic marital love is like a shield that protects the integral growth of a child. A child who is confident that Mom and Dad love each other and that this committed and unbreakable love is what has welcomed

---

3. Congregation for Catholic Education, *"Male and Female He Created Them": Towards a Path of Dialogue on the Question of Gender Theory in Education* (February 2, 2019), 4. Vatican website: *www.vatican.va*.

him into the world is at home in reality. We are made to love and to be loved, and a child who experiences this love in his or her family relationships has a deep sense that everything makes sense, that there is a meaning and purpose to one's life and it is good. A young child will not articulate this sense but it is apparent in trusting relationships that despite difficulties and suffering, there is a fundamental sense in which all is well: "God's in His heaven—All's right with the world!"[4]

In defining the family as a *communio personarum* St. John Paul II was well aware that history is rife with examples that fall short of this ideal. He famously referenced this definition as a challenge: "Family, become what you are."[5] Not only do individual families approach or fall short of the ideal, but likewise various cultures throughout history are more or less reflective of the truth of the family.

Though none of us are perfectly able to abstract ourselves from our current cultural context, we can learn from stories of different cultural and family traditions,

---

4. Robert Browning, "Pippa's Song," 1841.

5. John Paul II, Apostolic Exhortation on the Role of the Christian Family in the Modern World *Familiaris Consortio* (November 22, 1981), 17. Vatican website: *www.vatican.va*.

many of which shed light on particular aspects of our nature as embodied persons, male and female.

These anthropological truths are fundamental for understanding what a young child needs from his parents and family:

- **A Healthy Family.** A child receives most of what he or she needs from the family, not only basic material needs but also what he or she needs to thrive on a deeper level that includes emotional, intellectual, and spiritual dimensions. This naturally happens; it is "automatic" in a love-filled home. The love of Mom and Dad, both for each other and for the child, provides an ideal environment for the child's personality to begin to develop. Even before the child can speak or understand language, he or she is learning profound lessons about reality from the love of Mom and Dad. It is liberating for anxious parents to realize that there is no need to worry about whether they are giving their children what they truly need. Well before they study psychology books to understand in detail the different developmental stages and the markers of success for each stage, parents can already have great confidence that by following God's plan for the family they are participating in creating the right environment for their children to develop. Parents can leave their anxiety behind and instead focus on growing in love for God and each other, knowing that the result will be great good for their children as well.

THE MOTHER

A close physical relationship with Mom contributes to a deep sense of trust, not only in their mother's love, but that reality makes sense. Children do not understand in words that they have been created as dependent creatures that need not only physical nourishment but also relational connectivity to other persons, and ultimately to God. But these needs are built into human nature and are real even in a newborn baby.

For a newborn, the mother's role is primary. Physical contact is important and is naturally facilitated by the need for frequent feedings. Breastfed babies experience lots of close skin-to-skin contact, and bottle-fed babies are typically held closely as well. Breastfeeding naturally brings up questions from the other children—a great opportunity to explain the complimentarity of men, women, and their bodies, at the appropriate age level. As babies grow and begin to make eye contact, Mom's smile as well as the chance to be present, face-to-face, communicates a personal connection. The first months of life lay the foundation for, and begin the integral development of, one's personality.

THE FATHER

The father also has an important role to play in the early months of life. In the months before birth a baby begins to hear things. The child will come to know the comforting sound of mother's heartbeat. Of distant sounds, the most significant for a baby may be the father's voice. In some way, his voice can come to represent the outside world, which to a baby is vaguely understood as that which is "other." Perhaps there is a positive reaction on Mom's part in response to this voice that the baby picks up. An obstetrician once told me that he has observed many newborn babies stop crying, at least for a few seconds, when they first hear Dad's voice.

The father's voice is formative for babies in the first few months. Babies will be accustomed to their mother's gentle voice, a voice that takes a particular character and intonation when speaking to them. When Mom addresses Dad, her voice is different. She addresses in a different but loving way the one whose voice is "other," in some way symbolizing the outside world to the child. The response of this masculine voice, respected and welcomed by Mom, conveys the beginning of an understanding of the world as safe.

When Dad also holds and lovingly talks to his babies he conveys in a new and more direct way a welcoming world outside Mom's nurturing sphere. By his affection, Dad invites his babies to discover and become more open to the world, to journey from the maternal womb toward the eventual discovery of their place in the world. Later Dad will further this process in many ways, such as when he discusses, perhaps at the dinner table, his work or some world event in a realistic and yet optimistic way.

- **Arguments between Parents.** Spouses will argue and at times these arguments may be rather heated. This is not necessarily a big deal, so long as each comes to a better understanding of the other's perspective and there is forgiveness and charity going forward. Heated arguments between parents, however, should not take place in front of the children. This is true even when children are very young, or even not yet born.

The discord conveyed by Mom and Dad strongly arguing is jarring to the way the child understands reality. A young child lacks the experience and perspective to understand that parents can passionately argue but still love and respect each other. Instead, the heated argument, from the perspective of the child, is easily seen as threatening the love and unity that should be at the heart of the family. A child perceives heated parental discord as a personal threat to the family as a fundamental source of his or her identity. This can become more complicated if the child assumes that he or she is somehow responsible for what is wrong with mom and dad. Granted, young children may not be able to verbalize any of this. Even so, indistinct perceptions can still impact a developing personality.

This is not to say that Mom and Dad need always agree in the presence of their children. It is fine and even healthy for them to disagree in a polite and even cheerful way about all kinds of things. This can serve to highlight healthy differences in their personalities. It can be fun for children to see Mom and Dad cheer for different sports teams and a cordial, rational discussion about differing viewpoints on the merits of a book can be a good example of adults disagreeing without being disagreeable.

Substantial parental arguments will undoubtedly be less frequent and less serious if there is a regular time when the couple can get together to discuss family business, in a planned and somewhat professional way. These "business meetings" between husband and wife are excellent opportunities for reflecting together on each child and its development and growth in virtue. Husbands and wives often have different and complementary insights.

THE FAMILY STORY

Young children enjoy stories. Even before they can say more than a few words they will happily look at picture books, turning the pages of "board books" themselves. It is a real treat for them if Mom, Dad, a sibling, or another family friend "reads" such books to them. Sitting on a lap, youngsters point to different things in the pictures while the adult or older child names the object. As they get a bit older, they begin to understand narratives, simple stories of animals or families. Young children seem to enjoy hearing about routine events almost as much as unexpected adventures. It is delightful for adults to see toddlers enjoying hearing about *Goldilocks and the Three Bears* and other such tales.

Stories begin to expand the child's horizons, building up what is aptly called the moral imagination. A question begins to form, at first in an indistinct way, the beginning of a question that all mature people ponder: What type of story am I living? What is my place and role in this world and what does it all mean? These musings, however nebulous, provide parents an opportunity to convey details about the family story in a way that will ground a child's understanding of human love.

Parents should each tell from their own perspective about how they met and fell in love; Dad about the virtues he saw in Mom, her qualities that won his heart and how happy he was when she said yes to his marriage proposal. Mom should do the same, speaking in a loving way about the man she came to admire. Children will become very interested in hearing the details of this story, how Dad proposed, where they lived, the period of engagement, the wedding (girls especially want to hear about this) and the beginning of married life. As with other stories, this is one that will end up being told many times and perhaps different details will emerge each time. There is no need to force the telling of this story. Just be willing to tell it alongside the many other stories that are told in the family. Children will ask for it when they are ready and need to hear it.

Although telling the family story seems like such a natural, ordinary thing, apparently of little significance, it conveys deep truths. Young hearts, intrigued by all types of stories and wondering what type of story they are living, are met with a vision of human love and of the family as good and part of what grounds its place in the world. Human love is seen as leading toward marriage, toward the family. Masculinity and femininity complement and order this plan. A parent mentioning God in this context, just by noting thankfulness to God for one's spouse, reinforces the message that marriage and family are part of God's plan for us, something He built into human nature and has raised through grace, and certainly not something we humans invented.

MASCULINITY AND FEMININITY

Life begins and is nurtured in the mother's womb. Babies first hear the mother's sounds: her heartbeat and her voice, perhaps as she sings while doing simple tasks. Of all the sounds in the outside world, the father's voice is likely the most significant, as a voice that elicits a response from Mom, a response informed by love. Is it not reasonable to assume that, even from the womb, babies sense Mom's reaction and thus recognize that their father's voice is also significant? The father represents the outside world while the mother is seen as that which is intimate to their being. In the womb babies may only vaguely sense, if at all, the distinction between themselves and Mom.

Newborns' cries express the natural separation from Mom that occurs at birth. And while these cries can be temporarily stopped by the father's voice (can we perceive a small sense of wonder in newborns as they hear this voice already recognized as "other"?) it is when infants are placed on top of Mother's breast that calmness returns. Infants hear the familiar heartbeat and experience the known again in a comforting way. And so begins a series of short separations from Mother. Babies fall asleep breastfeeding and then wake up from their nap alone, cry, and are shortly picked up again. A baby's perception of self as a distinct person grows. An understanding of self and mother as distinct gradually solidifies.

Babies come to know that, like Father, Mother is also "other." As this process plays out their perception of Mom's nurturing femininity and Dad's strong and protective masculinity deepens. There comes a point when children come to know themselves as "a girl like Mom" or "a boy like Dad." This healthy process is naturally supported by normal family interactions.

It is not possible to talk about all the interactions that contribute to the good of children's discovery of self as male or female. I will only mention a few things that may be helpful.

PHYSICAL PLAY WITH DAD

On the positive side, dads should play with their toddlers in a physical way. Children who are gently tossed into the air and caught by their father's strong arms are playfully connecting with Dad and learning that masculine strength is meant to protect. Their father's strong arms convey that the world is good and we have a place in it. Mom should be nurturing and both parents should enjoy taking their toddlers on walks outside, validating their excitement in pointing to and naming things as they learn about the world.

- **Anger.** Both parents need to avoid displays of anger in front of the children. Parental anger can easily damage the parent-child relationship, weakening the child's trust in his mom or dad. Over time this will likely lead to a loss of self-confidence as well. Anger can also interfere with a child's growing sense of gender. If Mom is overbearing and harsh it will be more difficult for her children to understand and value the nurturing and life-giving side of femininity. A father's anger alarms a toddler who is trying to process what such anger means. If a young boy sees his father's anger as a threat, especially a threat to Mom, he may reject the masculine and over-identify with Mom as the nurturer and protector. A young girl regularly witnessing the anger of Dad is in danger of rejecting or misconstruing masculinity. In the extreme, a father's anger makes it more difficult for both his sons and daughters to grow up identifying with their biological gender and properly valuing the other gender.

Mom can help children process an outburst from Dad by the way she responds. If she responds with anger or fear, she validates that his outburst is a problem, making things more difficult for her child. If she remains calm and finds a way to tell her child that Dad is good (making excuses borne of charity and understanding), the child will tend to overlook the outburst and move on. Perhaps she could smile and say something like, "Daddy has been working hard at his job to take good care of us. He is so good to us even when things are difficult." This response will help the child not reject masculinity but rather grow in understanding that we are all complicated creatures.

It should be noted that this only works for the occasional angry outburst from Dad in the context of a husband and wife trying to live out God's plan for marriage and family. It is a short-term solution to an occasional outburst. A mother should not blame herself for her inability to make up for her husband's more serious anger problems. Likewise, at times the roles can be reversed, with the husband needing to respond charitably to an outburst from his wife. Although the dynamic involving masculinity and femininity may be somewhat different in this case, the effect of a calm and understanding charity is similarly able to smooth over what otherwise could lead to complications. And we do well to keep in mind that the tapestry of one's life is made up of many influences and people process experiences differently, sometimes even growing up well-adjusted in difficult family situations. Perhaps another relative, an uncle or grandfather, models healthy masculinity, or a grandmother or aunt femininity, in a way that compensates. Some children will be able to get what they need from healthy images of masculinity and femininity in good literature. However, parents should see significant anger, if it exists, as a major problem and should seek help.

CONNECTIONS

Though not as jarring as anger, emotional distance from a parent can complicate growing up. While Mom needs to be nurturing and motherly, Dad needs to be present and emotionally-engaged with each of his children. Problems in this area are commonly the result of distant fathers, who let their wives manage the affairs of the home and unfortunately do not make time for personally connecting with each child. The emotional distance of a father who retreats behind some device (or too much alcohol, or marijuana, etcetera) instead of being attentive to those around him is a much more serious problem than a father separated by mere physical distance. A father who is deployed with a military unit can still be very much emotionally present, even if only by a few weekly written lines remembering each child. For example, a note to his son congratulating him on the fort he built in the backyard (Mom sent a picture) and his loose tooth, along with an expressed desire to pass the ball together when he returns, goes a long way. Some men think that their role as "provider" is what's most essential. This can be farther from the truth. Although the family's financial wellbeing is certainly important, the spiritual, emotional, physical, and mental health of the family is equally the father's responsibility as the mother's.

Even a deceased parent can still be present if remembered and mentioned by the other. As a young boy, St. John Paul II commented that his mother remained present through the loving memory and words of his father.

MODESTY

We have been describing how it is primarily through healthy relationships with Mom and Dad that children learn the meaning of their existence as male or female persons. While these relationships are fundamental, teaching children appropriate social behavior is also important. Good manners help a person to concretely live in a way that appropriately expresses masculinity or femininity.

Young children lack a sense of discretion, a sense that everything they are thinking or feeling does not need to be displayed in public. This is painfully obvious to parents. Despite their best efforts, it is not uncommon for parents to find themselves leaving a public gathering, such as a religious service, with screaming toddlers upset because their will was contradicted in some apparently trivial way. We once were embarrassed when our then three-year-old son decided to discuss private parts at the dinner table while the pastor of our church was visiting. Another embarrassing moment occurred when our daughter, twirling around in her dress, decided to pull her dress all the way up, showing her undergarments, while visitors were over. Even though parents do well to laugh at these foibles, the innocent immaturity that is behind a child's lack of discretion reflects the need for a mature sense of custody of self, an ownership and guarded possession of what is most intimate to ourselves.

Mature masculinity and femininity are best expressed in a refined way, a way opposed to ostentatious displays. Refinement shows itself through many behaviors: table manners, pace of eating, waiting patiently for others, sobriety, and mortification, for example. It also shows itself through the actions and presentation of the body's masculinity or femininity. A man who acts overly macho is thought of as more like a barbarian than a gentleman. An overly flirtatious woman, revealing too much by her actions and dress, falls short of displaying a true image of feminine strength. A mature heart is one that is guarded and under that person's own dominion.

Mature masculinity and femininity is also best expressed through chastity. Chastity is the virtue that enables the self-possession characteristic of someone with dominion over the heart. This self-possession makes possible the authentic gift of self, in both small ways—countless daily acts of service—and in a more complete way, through a committed marital relationship or a celibate vocational commitment. Modesty is a virtue that helps to protect and express chastity. It is in the school of learning modesty that young children begin to journey toward the ideal of chaste love.

Parents teach modesty and decency by their example and by how they direct their children in specific situations. Parents should set a good example in how they dress both around the home and when going out. While it is fine to dress more comfortably around the home, efforts made to set a positive tone are not wasted. A man who, for example, typically wears pants and a collared polo shirt around the home is, over time, sending a dignified and respectful message to his sons and daughters. If he walks around without a shirt on he sends a different message. When going out in public, parents should dress in a way that is appropriate for the situation, even making efforts at times to elevate the tone. In other words, decorum is connected to modesty.

Parents do well to encourage their young children to keep their clothes on when going around the house. A young boy who wears shorts or pajama pants to bed should be encouraged to wear a shirt before coming for breakfast. Teenage boys may also need to be reminded on this point. Little girls wearing dresses and skirts may inadvertently display their undergarments, by how they move around when playing and by how they sometimes sit. It is good for parents to prompt their awareness and perhaps avoid this by encouraging them to wear, for example, bike shorts underneath. As girls get older it can seem more difficult to find modest clothing, although efforts to do so are well worth it. If a girl wants to wear something too revealing, she might be less receptive to guidance from her mother than from her father.

A father should reinforce the good criteria of modesty that a mother gives to her daughter, coming to an agreement on the criteria ahead of time and, together, warmly holding to it without absolutizing every detail. If it is necessary to send a strong message in this area, a father could say something like, "I do not like the way that outfit makes you look," or even stronger, "That outfit is going to make boys look at you in the wrong way."

Some teenage girls think more about how they will look to other girls than about how they will look to boys. Many girls are unaware of the effect that immodest clothing can have on boys; guidance from a father can help them to understand. Other teenage girls are aware of their effect on boys and like the attention it gives them; this lack of holistic self-esteem must be corrected. Hearing from their father about how they look to men can be shocking and repulsive, helping to open their eyes to the necessity for dressing in a more modest way.

Girls must also be aware that they have the power to set the tone around them, for example in the language, tone, and topic of their conversations. This can have a big impact on how boys treat them.

Modesty is, of course, not reserved for teenage girls. Boys must also be aware of the message they impart through their presentation. Teenage boys can tend to "show off" through their gestures and clothing choices. An example of this could be the cross-country boys who run through the neighborhoods with their shirts off, as if they are on a beach, not appropriate to the environment around them. Regardless of gender, our children must learn the value of modesty for themselves and for those around them.

CHAPTER 2

Conversations and Perspective

Well-chosen stories set the stage for conversations about marriage and the love between a man and a woman. Many children's books have rich images of noble human love. The brave knight, for example, must first defeat the dragon before marrying the princess. Or stories about a family of happy squirrels living in their cozy tree, and a frontier farming family living in the log house Pa built, present images of family unity and cooperation. If children are familiar with wholesome presentations of family life in stories, then it is natural for Mom and Dad to tell the story of their own families. Children will enjoy hearing such stories, learning about what it was like for Mom and Dad to grow up with their siblings and parents, the children's grandparents. They will especially like to hear, as previously mentioned, how Mom and Dad met, fell in love, were married, and joyfully welcomed the children God sent.

Conversations about the love between a man and a woman will be very simple at first. Children may ask basic questions about marriage and families. They may wonder why their aunt and uncle do not have children, to which a parent can respond that sometimes God does not bless a marriage with children because he has another plan for that couple. "And see how much good your aunt and uncle do by generously giving their time to help those who need it." Children may wonder about those who are not married, such as their parish priest or other single adults. Keeping in mind that many single adults are called to marriage, parents can explain that God has wonderful plans for some people that do not involve getting married. It is a great blessing to be called to serve God and others through a vocation as a single person.

And while children perceive the goodness of family life from the love in their own homes, parents will do well to explicitly mention that marriage and family life are part of God's plan and that this plan is very good. "God has everything so well planned.

He set up the family knowing that children need the love of a mother and a father."

Although even the very young learn about God indirectly through the way Mom and Dad live, care for them, and speak about the Mother of God, the angels, Jesus, the Father, and the Holy Spirit, when they become old enough to start learning about the faith and values of their home, parents should play a role in their catechetical instruction. Many children enjoy memorizing lists and practicing saying them out loud, perhaps as part of an evening routine. If they are memorizing the Ten Commandments, for example, parents can mention how some of these commandments directly refer to God's plan for marriage and family life. "Honor your father and mother" is an obvious one that applies directly to children's experiences. Less directly related are the sixth and ninth commandments about spouses being faithful to the exclusive nature of marital love between a husband and wife. Young children's understanding of the love between a man and a woman is mostly indirect; it is based on their experience of Mom and Dad's love for each other, rather than on a direct experience of movements of the heart, of attraction.

At some point, children encounter examples of things that are contrary to their own family life and the ideal of noble marital love. They will encounter examples of people living in irregular situations, perhaps even relatives. They see examples of a very different understanding of human sexuality. Some children's books attempt to normalize divorce or same-sex relationships. Film is a powerful medium and it is not uncommon for a child to see problematic content on a screen, even in homes where parents are careful. Children may also encounter more complicated situations from neighbors.

In one sense none of this is new. History is full of examples of everything from individual marital infidelity to systemic cultural immorality, such as the institution of pagan temple prostitution in the ancient world, or the portrayal in the Book of Genesis of the men of Sodom banging on Lot's door and demanding that he turn over what appear to be young male visitors.

But a case can be made that some of what is happening now is new and uniquely modern, inasmuch as it is a radical challenge to the acceptance of the reality of a natural order, including human nature, the givenness of persons being created male and female. The early modern setting aside of formal and final causality, beginning as an elite intellectual movement with such figures as Francis Bacon and René Descartes,[1] is playing out today on the level of popular culture, specifically in the tendency to reduce *natura*, including human nature, to a mere set of passive functional units subject to unlimited technological manipulation.[2] In modern thought and for many people today, things do not have set natures with characteristic perfections. Indeed, many today lack the patience to contemplate what a thing is and how it reveals itself in its actions. Instead, they are more interested in how a thing is constructed so as to devise ways to manipulate it. On a broad scale, this makes it possible to see human nature as malleable, as definable by the "collective" in the case of communism or by the needs of the state to create the "new

---

1. Though, as Étienne Gilson argues, Descartes may be better understood as attempting to respond to a climate of skepticism rather than intentionally being subversive.

2. It is interesting and, I think, worthwhile to ponder the difference between a modern reductive view of nature and the classical view articulated by Aristotle, "Nature is a principle and cause of being at motion and of being at rest that is in the thing to which it belongs primarily, and in virtue of itself, and not incidentally." Aristotle, *Physics* 2.1, 192b21–23.

man" in the case of fascism. In postmodern thought, one's identity is closely connected with a personal decision to identify with a specific group.

Our culture is changing fast, and the postmodern transgenderism of today may soon be dwarfed by a growing transhumanism movement, which seeks a new evolutionary stage ushered in by the future event known as "the singularity," where a merging of man and machine leads to a more powerful and potentially-immortal cyborg creature capable of self-regeneration. But it would be foolish for anyone to claim to know what the future holds on this score. It may well be that things will take a completely different turn more in accord with the truth about human nature and marital love.

But the point stands that the current situation is difficult and it is next to impossible for children growing up today to avoid encountering an attempt to normalize something directly contrary to God's plan for human love, marriage, and family. Wise parents will address these problems from a perspective of faith, helping their children to understand what type of story we are living, and where evil fits into this story. They will keep "the big picture" in mind so they have the right context for answering questions that arise.

GETTING THE BIG PICTURE RIGHT

We live in a world that is fundamentally good, as created by God. All evil and suffering in the world is the result of sin, which is a failure to use the awesome gift of freedom to love rightly. Evil is not on the same level as good; it is always a twisting of a good thing, never a creative force in itself. Evil is parasitic.

God only allows evil to exist because he is bringing a greater good from it. And he does not do things by half measures. When our first parents rebelled God did not intend merely to restore what was lost. From the love and perfect freedom of the Trinity, Father, Son, and Holy Spirit, came a plan for redemption so radical that it dwarfs the evil of sin, using this evil as a means for an even greater good. It is as if God the Son turned to the Father and the Holy Spirit and eagerly volunteered to become man and endure his passion to win a victory so great that we can exclaim with the Church at the Easter Vigil that what was lost through sin has been more than made up for in Christ: "O happy fault, O necessary sin of Adam, which gained for us so great a redeemer!"[3] We are truly made to be children of God through a

---

3. *Exultet* of the Easter Vigil liturgy.

participation in the inner life of the Trinity. Even in this life, beginning with Baptism, we are drawn into the inner life of God through Jesus Christ. This is the true story that we need to pass on to our children. And though we do well to tell this story directly, it comes to take root in children as they consider it in the context of personal experience and other stories.

Children are naturally open to transcendence. A young child looks at the world with questioning wonder, and recognizes its goodness. Materialism and other reductive patterns of thought are foreign to how children initially see reality. They are amused by the simplistic materialist view of reality displayed, for example, by Harry Potter's "muggle" relatives who express indignation at, and forceful opposition to, anything out of the ordinary.[4] The notion that authentic education is about "college and career readiness" so as to live comfortable muggle lives is repugnant to children. They would much rather study at Hogwarts, which is why the focus on information, text, and data

---

4. The *Harry Potter* series by J. K. Rowling does a good job critiquing, through the ridiculous behavior of the Dursley family, contemporary materialistic culture. It does a less adequate job in accurately conveying the transcendent struggle between good and evil. Rowling does a more helpful job presenting a compelling vision of evil than she does presenting the good.

analysis through the Common Core-aligned curriculum, which sets one set of academic expectations for all students regardless of their individualities, is so uninspiring. An authentic liberal arts education is much more in line with what children really need.

For materialists, the reality of evil in the world around us—and in our own hearts—is a danger lurking in the background that threatens to disrupt their comfortable existence. Just as children readily dismiss such materialism they also tend to accept at face value that the struggle between good and evil is a part of life. They are not scandalized by the fact of evil. In the face of the obvious goodness in the world it makes sense that there also be evil. Tales of heroism resonate with children who are open to the possibility of doing something great with their lives. Good children's literature appeals to a sense of life as an adventure, as a heroic quest where the protagonist is in one sense powerless against cosmic forces but who nonetheless plays out his part. The question that arises in young hearts is not whether good and evil exist, but rather how they fit into reality, how they relate to each other, and what a person's role is in the cosmic struggle between these forces that are beyond us.

The most simplistic and ultimately inadequate answer is that good and evil are two diametrically opposed forces battling in the arena of the universe. The *Star Wars* saga embodies this Manichean paradigm. On the positive side, there is the realization that a transcendent battle is raging around us and that we cannot ultimately remain neutral players; we must enter the fight. On the negative side is the notion that we become players in this conflict by a simplistic alignment with the "light side of the Force" used by Jedi knights. St. Augustine spent some time as a Manichean until he realized that evil is properly understood as a privation, as a corruption of a good thing by a voluntary turning toward a lesser good in a disordered way.

Fairy tales tend to point toward a better understanding of the relationship between good and evil.[5] The imaginative world of fairyland, manifested in different ways in particular tales, presents a moral and metaphysical landscape that rings true with human experience. For example, small children journey through an enchanted

5. Compilations by Andrew Lang are a good source of fairy tales. The work of George McDonald is also recommended. Be warned that many fairy tales are rather bizarre and may not seem beneficial. It might be more accurate to note that at their best traditional fairy tales are able to help form the moral imagination as discussed here.

wood characterized by strong forces far beyond their strength. Though the evil hag is terrifying, the children find safety while in the good fairy's presence, knowing that her power is greater by far. And though she will send them on a quest for the lost ring, as long as they remain true to her instructions, all will turn out well.

Fairy tales reference not only the transcendent struggle between good and evil, but also present a moral universe where good is more powerful and not threatened by evil in an ultimate sense. Grimms fairy tales, and others like them, put children on notice that in this world there are evil actors and evil actions, yet do so in a way that is appropriate to their age and maturity. While virtue and goodness wins, the fairy tales resemble the true Christian story we are living.

APPLICATIONS TO PRACTICAL SITUATIONS

The role of a good parent or teacher is to convey two clear points about good and evil to their children. First, with the help of good literature, they will emphasize that we are living in the midst of a transcendent battle between good and evil and the stakes could not be higher. The earthly happiness and eternal destiny of souls depends on how we live our lives. Second, our role in the cosmic battle between good and evil, though important, is a secondary one. God is ultimately the one in charge. Evil is not a separate force that is independent from God's providence. As a privation, a corruption of what was created good, a corruption rooted in the willful claiming of what is good as one's own apart from the way it is given by God, evil is merely parasitic. God would not allow evil unless he were able to draw an even greater good from it. We know that the grace of God embraced by those striving to live their vocations leads to the great good of being friends of God. This great good of freely loving God and others, both here in this life and in the next, far outweighs the cost of our being given this freedom in the first place.

Wise parents will continue to go back to these truths to help their children make sense of the evil they will inevitably encounter. Children will learn about parts of the world where people live in extreme poverty, suffering from hunger on a daily basis. They may witness signs of environmental damage nearby and learn about large-scale environmental problems associated with industrial processes. They will hear about crimes committed and learn about wars that may be happening now or have happened in the past. They may come in contact with individuals who are suffering from diseases, some very serious. And they may hear about victims of natural disasters like earthquakes.

For the most part parents can place contemporary attacks on God's plan for human love, marriage, and family in this context. Children can readily understand that the devil is working to cause havoc in these areas, precisely because God's plan is so good. At first, parents may simply mention the fact that marriage and the family are under attack today, and nightly prayers can include praying for families. As children see things that are disordered parents can explain how these disorders relate to the devil's attack on marriage and family. If parents do this in the right way they will model an appropriate response for their children.

In specific cases it can be difficult for children to understand sound principles for judging right from wrong and yet not fall into making rash judgments about people in particular circumstances. It's hard enough for adults! Problems related to marriage and family tend to require more maturity than other clear manifestations of evil such as violence in war. A child may learn that the couple living together next door is not married yet but are thinking about getting married at some time in the future. A parent would do well to encourage their child to pray for them and even to mention some of the virtues that their neighbors possess. "It was kind and generous of Bill and Betty to shovel the snow off our walk while we were out of town. They really go out of their way to be good neighbors." This will set the stage for helping to provide the correct perspective. In response to their child asking why Bill and Betty are not married, a parent could respond with something to the effect of,

> Many people, through no fault of their own, are confused about what God's plan for marriage and family even means. We need to pray, set a good example, and occasionally, at the right time, rely on the Holy Spirit to help us say the right things.

The key is to convey a sense that many people of good will simply do not understand what is going on. Granted, there are a few clever people whose views should be countered by professionally-competent and well-formed men and women,[6] but

6. An excellent example of doing just this is the following presentation on gender questions from the Witherspoon Institute: Dr. Ana Samuel,

the majority around us are struggling to find their way. We will win them over by prayer and kindness. We should always assume the best about others and keep in mind the inherent dignity of every human being, as they search for the truth.

PROBLEMS IN THE CHURCH

At some point children are going to hear about the serious moral failures of various Church officials, whether priests, bishops, or cardinals. Since the Church is a divine institution founded by Jesus Christ, it would be a serious mistake to present the Church as merely a human institution, as a way of excusing these actions. Striking the right balance is not easy for parents and educators.

Parents may say, in their own words, something along these lines:

> The war between good and evil in our world is very much present in the Church as well. It is important to remember that God's plan is still working and

---

"Sex, Gender and Identity," July 12, 2018, The Witherspoon Institute, video, *https://winst.org/ana-samuel-sex-gender-identity/*.

that we could be witnessing a time of purification that is the beginning of a great new era of holiness and apostolate emerging from the heart of the Church. It is fundamentally a good thing that the evil works of some people come to light as it provides an opportunity for the Church to be purified.

In talking with children it is best to understate outside attempts to infiltrate the Church. It is enough for them (and probably for us as well) to know that there are enemies aligned with the devil whose efforts to infiltrate the Church are partly responsible for the confusion and problems we are witnessing today.[7]

It is unfortunately true that some of the problems in the Church today are widespread; there are places where dissent from Church teachings is the norm. Even so, the Church possesses the fullness of the means of salvation and Christ has guaranteed she will persevere until the end of time. If we should help foster a healthy patriotism in our children regarding this imperfect yet fundamentally good country in which we live, so much more should we strive to foster a love

---

7. See Philip Puella, "Pope Blames Devil for Church Divisions, Scandals, Seeks Angel's Help," Reuters, October 8, 2018, *https://www.reuters.com/article/topNews/idCAKCN1MI10M-OCATP?edition-redirect=ca.*

for our Holy Mother the Church. And we should remember that this is not the first time in her history that widespread dissent and confusion has been overcome by the truth. When the Arian heresy appeared to have triumphed, only a few stood firm fighting for the divinity of Christ: St. Athanasius of Alexandria in the East, apparently standing "against the world," and later St. Hilary of Poitiers in the West.

ABORTION

Of all the evils in the world that children may encounter or learn about, the evil of abortion is different, both because of what it is and because of the way it is hidden from view. Abortion is an overwhelming evil that is difficult to fathom, even for adults. There are, of course, heart-wrenching scenarios some women face upon learning about an unexpected pregnancy. Not least among the sufferings women and men face is coming to understand what has happened to their aborted child, how their child felt pain and perhaps attempted to flee from the surgical implements that ended his or her life. It is difficult to know what to say to someone who is grieving over a child lost to abortion.

The scale of this institutionalized evil is overwhelming. In the United States alone approximately one out of every five pregnancies ends in abortion, amounting to about one million deaths per year.[8] Though the United States has a high rate of abortion compared to most of the rest of the world, it is by no means the country with the highest rate.[9]

While it is difficult for adults to think about this great evil, it is particularly challenging for children, especially the first time they realize what is happening. Children are trusting by nature and are disposed to think well of people serving in various professions, including all medical professionals. It can be profoundly jarring for a child to realize that such a widespread destruction of human life is taking place in clinics and hospitals throughout our country, supported

---

8. See "U.S. Abortion Statistics: Facts and Figures Relating to the Frequency of Abortion in the United States," Abort73.com, Loxa famosity Ministries, Inc., accessed October 14, 2021, *https://abort73.com/abortion_facts/us_abortion_statistics/*.

9. "Unintended Pregnancy and Abortion Worldwide," Guttmacher Institute, July 2020, *https://www.guttmacher.org/fact-sheet/induced-abortion-worldwide*; and "Worldwide Abortion Statistics: Facts and Figures relating to the Incidence of Abortion Worldwide," Abort73.com, Loxa famosity Ministries, Inc., accessed October 14, 2021, *https://abort73.com/abortion_facts/worldwide_abortion_statistics/*.

by and carried out by healthcare workers who should be serving the common good. A band of brigands leaving their secret lair in the forest to prey upon innocent travelers is much more comprehensible to a child than babies being killed in their mothers' wombs in a medical facility by doctors and nurses. How should parents help their children make sense of this?

The first point is that the horror of abortion is so great that it is not unreasonable for parents to avoid explaining this evil to children until it is necessary to do so. Children will hear the word "abortion," perhaps even at church when general prayers are offered for "an end to abortion." Similarly, it is not wrong for parents to mention "the defense of human life" or even more directly "an end to abortion" as intentions during family prayers. As with many other things, however, years can go by without a youngster actually realizing what is going on. Parents should not push young children to become aware of the full reality behind these words.

At the same time, parents should be close enough to their children to realize when awareness begins to dawn. The tone taken by parents when talking about abortion and all evil to children is important. It is not uncommon for a children to become overwhelmed when they begin to understand the magnitude of the evil of abortion. A parent with a strong supernatural sense that God is ultimately in charge and that his purposes are being accomplished in history will be able to convey that in spite of the horrors of worldly evil, we can travel through this life as confident children. God is in charge and is bringing good out of all the evil that he allows to happen.

Parents should be calm without in any way making light of what is happening. It would be a critical mistake to be dismissive. It may be helpful to note that powerful forces of good and evil are sometimes hidden from plain view. Just as we may not realize the tremendous impact prayer has on history, or the extent to which angels are active, so the devil is pleased that some of his worst work remains mostly hidden, at least for a time. There were certainly blind spots of other passed eras. For example, the proliferation of slavery throughout America, let alone the rest of the world, was readily accepted as a norm by a great number of societies. Parents can use this example to explain that, although we have respect for the law of the land, societal law does not always reflect God's law. Parents can also point out that though abortion is so widespread throughout our country, most doctors and nurses have nothing to do with it. There are many pro-life medical professionals.

The hiddenness of evil allows many people to continue to live on a shallow level, going through life as if money and worldly power mattered more than they actually do. If the horror of the silent millions killed by abortion were frequently before each person's mind's eye, a graphic picture of the doctor's implements and the squirming child, it would be less possible to hide behind language like "women's health" and "reproductive rights."

PATRIOTISM

As children (and adults as well) begin to grasp the great evil of abortion, all the more striking for being hidden from view, they may fall into an overly negative view of our country. Doesn't the reality of great evil, protected by our legal system, mean that our country is utterly corrupt? To take the point further, there are those who use the ugliness of the reality of abortion as a way to manipulate others by creating a "package" of issues, one of which is abortion, the rest which constitute their opinions (and not intrinsic truth or Church teaching) on crime, education, health, and more. Parents should help children maintain a balanced view that includes room for genuine patriotism and thankfulness. The early Christians are an excellent model for us. Though the Roman Empire had many flaws, including persecutions of Christians and brutal public gladiatorial games, Christians strove to be good citizens, praying for the civil authority and recognizing that the civil authority acted mostly in accord with God's governance of the world. St. Paul is very clear on this (for example, see Rom 13:1–7).

It is not true that a country has to be great before it is loved; a country becomes great through the love and prayers of its citizens. There are undoubtedly problems with the United States and other countries, problems including but not limited to failure to defend the weakest and poorest human lives. But there is a great deal of good as well. We all owe a great debt of gratitude to this country and part of the way we show this gratitude is by exercising our role as citizens to work for solutions to problems within the context of a civil system that allows for this possibility.

CHAPTER 3

Teaching Your Young Children about Love

Conversations for young children are mostly about helping them to understand what type of story we are living. We hope that they begin to see the outlines of the great battle that is taking place between good and evil and how they are protected as children under the care of the best of fathers, God the Father himself. In this context some aspects of God's plan for human love, marriage, and family will begin to come up. Children will be growing in their understanding of the profound goodness of God's plan for the family and will also understand that forces of evil are on the attack. The details of the enemy's battle plan will be vague in children's minds, although they may have asked about some particulars and received age-appropriate answers from parents.

At the right time, parents should take the initiative and have the first of several intentional conversations.

While it makes sense to wait until a child is old enough for such a conversation to be meaningful, it is important for parents to do this before their child picks up a different understanding of these matters from other sources. If a child is home-schooled or in a particularly wholesome school environment, this might be able to wait until around third grade or even a bit later. For many children, it will be best for parents to have the first conversation earlier, in which case the content should be simplified to be age appropriate. On the one hand, parents should respect their child's innocence by not mentioning difficult content too early. On the other hand, it is important for parents to give their child enough guidance so that he or she is not shocked and caught off guard. A child will be more likely to recognize reductive views of sexuality as lies if he or she has first heard a more complete vision of human love from a parent. These conversations are best done father to son and mother to daughter. Here are some points that may be helpful.

CONTEXT

These are important conversations and it makes sense to prepare in advance. Early in the week a parent could mention a plan to get together, perhaps on Saturday afternoon, to go for a walk and talk about a few things. Children will likely want to know right then what the talk will be about. I would recommend not giving away too much. Just let them know that there are some things that fathers talk to their sons about and mothers talk to their daughters about and "since you are getting older it makes sense for us to talk." It might help to go to a private place away from home. This will add to the importance of the talk and help distinguish it from the many informal communications that take place at home.

CONTENT

Mention that you want to talk about God's plan for human love, marriage, and family. This is important. By referring to God's plan right from the start parents are emphasizing that they are not simply sharing personal thoughts. The reference to "God's plan" establishes a context that is broad and open to the full truth about human love, marriage, and family. This perspective is directly opposed to the limited reductive approaches that are unfortunately all too common, and easily fostered by language that overly focuses on the mechanics ("how babies are made" or "the birds and the bees"). Most contemporary problems in the area of sexual attraction have to do with reductionism, taking a part of something that is fundamentally good but isolating it from its proper context and magnifying certain aspects of experience in a way which risks objectifying the person. To focus primarily on mechanics is to reduce sexual relations to a function rather than seeing it in the proper context of a relationship.

Continue with general comments about things your child already knows: God's plan is very good, Mom and Dad are very happy to be trying to live according to God's plan, are very thankful for each other and for each of the wonderful children with which God has blessed the family, and that there is a battle taking place in the world around us to attack marriage and the family. And then, with refinement, explain that in God's plan a married couple comes together for the first time on their wedding night.

Use your own words to convey something like,

When a husband and wife come together it is a beautiful thing. God has made us so that as we grow older we see the attractiveness of a loving union between husband and wife that is expressed when they come together in the marital embrace. This is a great gift from God and is a wonderful part of marriage. Coming together in this way becomes a part of the husband and wife's life together and God uses this loving embrace to bless them with children. When a new baby is conceived in Mommy's womb, he or she begins growing right away. At first the baby is very small but soon will be big enough for us to notice. Some couples find it hard to have a baby. This does not mean that God does not love them, but rather that he has other plans for them at that time or even throughout their entire married life. It is also wonderful for someone to be called and given the grace to forgo marriage and live their life with a heart that is free to love God and others through a single vocation. Through such a single vocation a person can serve and help many families.

GOD'S PLAN UNDER ATTACK

A parent continues,

> This beautiful plan of God for human love, marriage, and families is under attack in some specific ways today. After sin, our hearts are disordered in their desires. We long for things and to possess them in wrong ways, in ways that are not in accord with God's plan. However, we are called to live the virtue of chastity by which we guard our hearts, not allowing them to form attractions in the wrong ways.
>
> As people get older and go through bodily changes called puberty they will also experience changes in their hearts. A boy may start noticing girls in a new way and vice versa. It is normal to experience these movements of the heart, accompanied by bodily sensations, but it is important to not act upon them, even interiorly. A young person could get the idea that these accompanying physical sensations themselves are evil instead

of being gifts of God to be integrated into life according to God's plan. Rather, see this capacity for human love as a great gift that God has given us, a gift that we must protect by keeping it guarded and protected until the right time.

Today there are people involved in trying to get others to look at the human body in the wrong way. They present images of people that try to make them look attractive in the wrong way. People are trying to get others to compromise their hearts, losing their chaste integrity. This happens through immodest pictures that are even present in public places like stores. It also happens with certain styles of clothing worn by some people, who often do not really know what they are doing.

Some people even produce some really bad materials, called pornography, which is designed to make someone a spectacle for sinful attraction. Many people get into trouble looking at pornography on computer screens because it is so easy to access. It is also addictive. People who get into the habit of viewing pornography not only offend God but they also make it difficult for themselves to love others rightly. Over time people can become perverted, twisted by the images they have consumed. Even so, they have hope for forgiveness and healing with God's grace.

PRACTICAL CONSIDERATIONS

It is fine if the first talk on these matters is fairly short. The purpose of this talk is not just to convey information but to establish yourself as the one your child can and should go to if he or she has any questions. If the tone of the talk is calm and positive the child will likely feel appreciative that mom or dad took the time to "treat me a bit like a grown up in talking to me not just as a parent but also as a friend." After you finish making the few points you intend to convey it is good to ask if your child has any questions. Questions should be answered simply and truthfully in an age-appropriate way. As a rule of thumb, it is usually best to give enough information to adequately answer the question that your child asked without going into details that are not necessary and perhaps would be too much for a young child to process. Children may not have any questions. If you ask if there are any questions and your child asks about something completely off topic, such as a question about baseball, you can consider this a success. Enough was covered for the first of these talks; no need to push it.

SUBSEQUENT TALKS

This initial talk should be the first of several similar talks that will take place as your child grows up. It is good to circle back for another planned discussion the following year or possibly sooner. A parent who is close to his or her child will have an idea if such a talk should take place sooner; living in a world in which it is impossible to miss so many false notions of love, it is likely. These subsequent talks should begin with the same foundational principles, outlined above, that were originally covered. It is even possible that your child may have mostly forgotten what you previously told him or her, or perhaps even somewhat forgotten that you even had that conversation at all. Children tend to absorb information for which they are ready; the rest can easily "go in one ear and out the other," as the saying goes.

Below are some topics that can be helpful to address in such subsequent conversations, when the child is ready.

- **Bodily changes.** Parents should alert their children to the changes that their bodies undergo through puberty. A father should mention to his son and a mother to her daughter some of the changes that will take place. It might feel like you are simply stating the obvious when you mention clear examples of physical development, such as additional hair growth or, in the case of women, the development of breasts. Your child has undoubtably already seen others develop physically from children to young adults in these ways. Beginning with a few obvious examples, however, can be a good way to introduce the more hidden bodily changes that take place. Likewise, a parent mentioning these changes can easily convey that these physical changes are good and according to God's plan, as well as make it easy for a child to ask questions about things that may otherwise be unclear.

A father should inform his son about nocturnal emissions, ideally before the first one happens. Let him know that God made the male body so that semen builds up and needs to be released. This happens at night and may or may not involve waking up. It might happen that one wakes up during a dream and senses something very pleasurable.* Give your son a heads up that the emission is likely going to be a bit messy and will require getting a clean pair of underwear. Assure him that it is not wrong to have a nocturnal emission.

A mother should likewise talk to her daughter about what going through puberty is like for girls. She will tell her daughter about the menstrual cycle of a grown woman and how this begins with the first period. Mention that though it can be surprising and even a bit unsettling when this happens for the first time, it is all part of God's good plan. Families tend to delay this talk, which leads to ten- or eleven-year-olds panicking at

---

* The pleasure is part of God's gift and, as such, is good. It is meant to accompany the marital act. It is wrong to seek this pleasure in isolation but this is not what happens in a nocturnal emission.

the onset of their period. Prepare your daughter with calm expectation. When the time is right, a mother can also show her daughter how to chart her monthly cycle in order to understand her fertility more in depth and to be ready for the start of her cycle each month.

- **Changes in one's heart.** Mentioning bodily changes can be a good way to segue into changes of the heart, perhaps along these lines,

> As one grows up, along with the bodily changes that take place, there are accompanying changes in the heart as well. There is a natural recognition of the attractiveness of being together with someone of the opposite sex.
>
> This attraction sheds a new light on the goodness of God's plan for marriage; the heart seems made for such a committed union. These changes in the heart, while fundamentally good, are not without complications. You know that we are made for much more than earthly happiness, that our vocation is to serve others and God in this life so as to find true happiness in the life to

come. Nothing in this world can satisfy the deepest longings of the human heart. The many good and pleasurable things in this life should be accepted as gifts from God pointing toward the true happiness that God wants for us, which is not possible in this world. We need to avoid coveting pleasures and experiences here as ends in themselves, ends we try to grasp according to the measure of our desires. The human heart should not seek to possess goods on its own terms, setting up desires and experiences as idols in place of God. Instead, the good things of this life hint at the greater good that awaits us in heaven if they are received with thankfulness according to God's plan.

A fundamental aspect of God's plan is that giving into movements of the heart that lead to sexual pleasure is only legitimate in marriage. To seek fulfillment of sexual desires outside of marriage is wrong; it is not according to the purposes of this wonderful relational capacity that God has built into our natures, the purpose being unity and procreation within marriage. Pleasure is a gift from God, but it is part of a *whole plan*; take away the rest of the plan, and pleasure becomes an idol. We need to live the virtue of chastity, by which we live with guarded hearts. Chastity enables the self-possession necessary to be able to give oneself to another as a gift. It is impossible to give what one does not have. Chastity is not the enemy of fulfillment in relationships but rather the virtue that enables love to deepen, to become more powerful and transformative. Where chastity is absent, love is debased and threatened.

The need for self-mastery is not unique to romantic relationships. During the US Civil War, some Union soldiers came across a still of moonshine, drank to excess, and were killed by a surprise rebel attack that night.[1] In giving into intemperance, they forgot about their mission. We need to have the presence of mind not to forget about God's designs for the human heart.

1. As presented in John J. Pullen, The Twentieth Maine: A Classic Story of Joshua Chamberlain and His Volunteer Regiment (Mechanicsburg, PA: Stackpole Books, 2008.])

It is wrong to give free reign to the desires
of the human heart, even in one's imagination. It is also seriously wrong to entertain
thoughts or engage in actions that cause sexual arousal outside of the context of the marital embrace. To deliberately seek or stimulate
sexual pleasure through impure thoughts or
actions is the sin of masturbation.[2] This is a
serious matter and one does well to mention
any such sin in confession prior to going to
receive our Lord in Holy Communion. Sometimes it is difficult to know for sure what one
intended and the extent to which there was
a deliberate seeking of something illicit. Try
not to become scrupulous. Our Lord is merciful and is very pleased with us when we
try to live the virtue of holy purity, when we
struggle in this area. Do not become complicated in trying to over-analyze all movements
of your heart. If there may have been some
consent just resolve to mention it in your next

---

2. See *Catechism of the Catholic Church*, 2nd ed., Washington, DC:
Libreria Editrice Vaticana–United States Conference of Catholic Bishops, 2000, 2352.

confession and move on. Carrying on an interior dialogue on such matters is rarely helpful.

- **React strongly when purity is at stake.**

  Where purity is at stake, so is the charity for which it aims. We are all called to be witnesses to the truth about human and divine love. We do this by the example we set, by living the virtues, and by keeping close to God through prayer and the sacraments. At times particular situations may arise that require decisive action. We should not tolerate any disrespectful speech about God's plan for human love, whether it is someone joking about something or saying something about a sexual matter in an inappropriate way. Sometimes the best thing to do will be to simply leave, and at other times it will be best to directly confront the person, perhaps saying something like, "I can't imagine you saying that about your mother, so I don't think you should be saying it about someone else's daughter either." If you find yourself in a situation where someone tries to show you some very bad images, what we talked about as pornography, you should always react strongly, by refusing to look at it or walking away. In some situations it might even be best to reach out and crumple the pornographic image and throw it down on the ground before walking away. These are effective ways to help the other person, your classmate for example, know how serious this is. If you do this I want you to know that I will always support you and take the blame if possible. Feel free to tell your classmate that if he has a problem with you destroying the pictures, that he should tell his dad to call your dad.

Pornography is a horrible thing and harms many people. It is intentionally made to get young people to take that second and then third look until they feel a strange sort of attraction to it. Pornography presents the human body in such a way as to arouse sexual desire outside of the intimate context of marriage that makes it good and holy. It is produced in order to entertain, to shock, to seduce. Pornography is not pornography because it shows too much of the human body, but rather because it shows too little of the human person. Some beautiful art-works by masters such as Michaelangelo show a person without clothing but are not pornographic. On the contrary, some pornographic images include some sort of clothing.

Your defense has to be to guard both your eyes and your heart. Just as you should refuse to look at any pornographic image someone directly tries to show you, you should also quickly and decisively turn away from any impure content that you happen to come across. Some of this content is right in public view. Look away. Say a prayer to our Lady. And if you do end up taking that second look or giving something more consideration than it deserves, mention it in your next confession. You will be given the graces to keep the fight far away from the interior sanctuary of your heart.[3] If you meet the enemy far away in these little details then you will be protecting the fortress of your heart.

Regardless of the exact words used, parents should bring up the topic of pornography in a

3. See Josemaría Escrivá, *The Way* (New York: Scepter, 1982), 307.

way that models for their children how to reject this great evil. Children should feel empowered to definitively reject pornographic content, knowing that they have full parental support. For example, if there is a pornographic television commercial, parents can tell the child that they should take the remote and change the channel without needing to seek permission. This allows your child to feel the responsibility. Again, Pornographic content is often designed to shock. Typical children, if they are not warned ahead of time, may not know how to process what is happening as these images are thrust into their view. They may be simultaneously repelled and attracted to what is seen. Interiorly, a problematic dialogue begins that is paralyzing to them. After a few seconds they may look away in disgust, but a dangerous seed has been planted. If parents mention that it is OK to violently react against this great evil, that doing so is justified and even noble, they will be spreading a strong protective shield over the children. And the children, rather than being frozen in a paralyzed stupor, will strongly and promptly reject the image with a sporting spirit, knowing that Mom and Dad have their backs.

- **Same-Sex Attraction.**

  Looking at pornography is one factor that can lead to the disordered situation where a man is sexually attracted to another man or a woman is sexually attracted to another woman. This is called same-sex attraction. Some people use the words "homosexuality" or "homosexual" or "gay" to describe this. One problem with these words is that they tend to imply that a person is defined by his sexual attractions, as if being homosexual were a defining characteristic of him as a person. We should never define a person according to his disordered sexual attractions and for this reason it is better to use the phrase "same-sex attraction."

  Another problem with these words is that it blurs the distinction between feelings, especially if non-consensual, and actions to which, presumably, consent is given. This is routinely ignored in our culture, and once lost, makes it difficult for the teenager with same-sex attractions to avoid being swept into a promiscuous gay subculture. The difference between "feelings" and "actions" is crucial; the absence of understanding this difference explains why Catholic morality comes across as opaque and nonsensical to many young people.

At times there are contributing factors that lead to same-sex attraction, and at other times there are no identifiable causes. Some same-sex attraction at certain ages is not atypical. It may simply be a passing phase for a young person. People who experience deep-seated same-sex attraction as adults have a particular cross to bear. Besides pornography, unhealthy past relationships can contribute to deep-seated same-sex attraction. Children who are abused are at a higher risk of developing same-sex attraction. It is important to understand that we need to be very charitable toward anyone who may be struggling with same-sex attraction.

God calls all people without exception to holiness, which includes living all of the virtues. All of us, including those with deep-seated same-sex attraction, are called to live the virtue of chastity. One type of chastity is proper to married men and women, in which husband and wife are called to love each other rightly. Another type of chastity helps someone live out a single vocation, which is not so much a denial of the longing for fatherhood or motherhood, but lifting it to a higher level.[4] The type of chastity that people with deep-seated same-sex attraction are called to live is more difficult in that it necessarily involves more self-denial. While it is possible for this brokenness to be partly or fully healed and order restored to the heart, some individuals may experience the cross of having deep-seated same-sex attraction. This cross means one must live a self-denial that unites the person to the Holy Cross that Christ carries.

---

4. There is a profound relationship between marriage and celibacy whereby both vocations are mutually supported. Through a celibate vocation for the kingdom one is available to serve many families, helping families strive for holiness and witnessing to the deepest meaning of love. Authentic married love likewise witnesses to selfless dedication through countless details of charity in spite of hardships endured.

There is a big difference between crosses of our own making that we endure without profit and sufferings that, united to our Lord, lead to a loving union with him. Such crosses are mostly carried by him and are compatible with great joy. As I said earlier, we must be very charitable toward those who may struggle with same-sex attraction, who will feel discouraged from mockery and cruel insults that make their cross more difficult to bear.

Although it is perhaps not a priority to mention to your child, it is worth keeping in mind that men with deep-seated same sex-attraction are not good candidates for the priesthood. The Church's teaching is that such men should not seek ordination.[5]

SIGNS OF CONFUSION

In addition to pornography and same-sex attraction, confusion exists about the meaning of male

---

5. Congregation for Catholic Eduction, Instruction *Concerning the Criteria for the Discernment of Vocation with regard to Persons with Homosexual Tendencies in view of their Admission to the Seminary and to Holy Orders* (August 31, 2005), 2. *Vatican website: www.vatican.va.*

and female. In creating persons as either male or female, God intends that they develop authentic masculinity or femininity, that they develop hearts that love with the strength and care of a father's heart or the kindness and tenderness of a mother's heart.[6] Some people think that one's gender is not fixed at birth as either male or female. People recognize that there are obvious differences between boys and girls at birth but see gender as something that someone should be able to change over time if they are not comfortable with their biological gender. Some people take medicine to help them look more like the opposite gender. They begin to dress and act like someone of the opposite gender.

Growing up is difficult for many people and it is not uncommon for someone to experience some confusion about who they are and are called to be. It is very sad when adults assist children experiencing this confusion in taking a step as drastic and serious as taking medicine to make them appear like the opposite sex. This change, or switch, is what the word "transgender" means.

---

6. Congregation for Catholic Education, "*Male and Female He Created Them*," 4, 11, and others.

The suffering leading someone to seek to identify with a different gender is often rooted in objective psychological and spiritual difficulties. Many are confused and think that undergoing a gender transition, or counseling someone to do so, promises relief and freedom. In actuality, the suffering is all to often made worse. Charity demands that we look on such situations and persons with compassion and never belittle those who are being sold gender transitions as a false solution.

Along with a view of gender as something we can manipulate rather than as a given part of who we are is a tendency to view gender as unimportant. It is certainly true that there should not be unjust discrimination in the workplace because of one's gender. Women should not be treated unfairly because they are women and there should be a recognition that masculinity and femininity are complementary. One is not more important than the other, although situations may call for strengths of a more feminine or masculine type. A woman can do a job in a feminine way and be just as effective as a man who does the same job in a more masculine way. For example, the motherly charity of a female medical doctor is just what some situations may require. And both male and female doctors can have warm bedside manners in ways that are particular to their masculinity and femininity, while at the same time making good rational medical decisions based on the same medical science. But we all are impoverished by a move toward a genderless mode where the good of both masculinity and femininity are missing.[7]

KEEP IT RELAXED

The above monologues are merely intended as examples of how such things could be covered. The intention is not to provide a conversation script. If a particular phrase strikes you as a good way to explain something feel free to use it after making it your own. What you say has to be in your own words and it has to ring true as warm parental advice from you to your child. Not everything needs to be addressed and certainly not all at one time. Omissions are not a big deal if your child feels comfortable going to you

7. Congregation for Catholic Education, "*Male and Female He Created Them*," 21.

with questions. If you notice that a conversation has covered enough then don't try to force more. Parents who discuss these things with their child will be conveying a positive message merely by taking the time to cover this material as the child's father or mother. Make sure your child knows that they can come back and ask any questions that may arise.

Parents should avoid talking about their own personal faults in this area. It is fine to mention that all of us are called to struggle, with God's grace, to have a pure heart. It is okay to mention in very general terms that you also have to struggle to keep the fight far away from the fortress.[8] If your child asks you about your past it is best to let them know that conversations about these matters are delicate. It is sensible to tell an overly inquisitive child that some questions are not appropriate to ask.

---

8. See Josemaría Escrivá, *The Way*, 307.

CHAPTER 4

—

Responding to Situations

Up to this point we have mostly been presenting a proactive approach that parents can take to properly form and educate their children. But as all experienced parents know, much of what we do is reactive rather than proactive. Situations arise that require a parental response, or at least a deliberate "non-response." Many more situations arise than is possible to discuss here. Here's some perspective for a few.

GENDER CONFUSION AMONG YOUNG CHILDREN

A young child may express interest in identifying with the opposite gender. Many children enjoy dressing up as a form of imaginative play. A two-year-old boy may want to wear dresses as he plays with his older sisters. He may even talk about being "pretty" and say things about being a girl or wanting to be a girl.

Sensible parents will avoid overreacting, realizing that they should not take anything a two-year-old does too seriously. It may be best to ignore the situation altogether. If cross-dressing becomes a habitual form of play, it may be appropriate for a parent to calmly tell the young lad that it is not good for boys to dress up as girls and make him take off the dress. Even if parents are privately concerned about such behavior it is important to stay calm and respond with clear expectations for how young boys should behave. If a consequence for disobeying is required such as a short "time out" it should be administered calmly and the focus should be on the need to obey Mom and Dad more so than on the behavior. Young girls may tend to want to dress and act more like boys. In most situations this does not need to be thought of as a problem at all.

The classic book *Caddie Woodlawn* by Carol Ryrie Brink portrays a frontier family whose listless and sickly daughter was allowed to play and roam with her brothers. Acting as a tomboy was just what she needed to regain her health and vivacity. Caddie comes to realize that while the rough and tumble ways of boys are fine, the more feminine side of being a girl is also good. She naturally tempers her tomboy side and begins to grow into a well-adjusted young woman.

Parents do well to allow their daughters to benefit from outdoor play, hiking, and sports just like their sons. Mothers also should teach them how to do domestic tasks such as cooking and taking care of a home. Young girls and boys tend to love baking projects with Mom. And while most young girls will enjoy wearing dresses, even those who favor more athletic clothing will have the chance to dress nicely for more formal and special occasions. Even a tomboy will probably enjoy learning about fashion if it is presented in an attractive way, perhaps as an afternoon course sponsored by a girl's club run by mothers.

YOUNG CHILDREN AND "PRIVATE PARTS"

Young children typically, albeit slowly, come to understand that certain body parts are meant to be treated with respect and even refinement. Parents reinforce this by encouraging children as young as two to keep their private parts covered. "Private parts are the areas covered by bathing suits—both girls and boys have private parts 'in the middle.'" But experienced parents know that young children have a tenuous understanding of modesty and decorum. They tend to express exactly what they are thinking or feeling, leading to some amusing anecdotes and antics. Young children may decide that they want to undress and run around the house naked. They may also decide to play with their "private parts."

Young boys and girls may fondle themselves, but parents should not overreact or draw conclusions too quickly. This does not mean that such behavior is normal and should be liberally tolerated by parents. Redirection and simple correction are very much in order. "Come here to Mommy. Time to get dressed again. It is good to keep private parts covered. We want to be modest." Or a father to a young son, "It's not polite to touch there. Let's go out outside, Daddy wants to show you something."

NEIGHBORHOOD SITUATIONS

Parents should encourage their children to be broad-minded, understanding, and tolerant of the faults of others. Charity requires that we strive to think well of others; even when we clearly witness actions contrary to God's ways, we should be quick to make excuses for the persons involved when possible. This fundamental openness to others enables us to accompany them with an offer of genuine friendship. Living this way helps all of us more deeply discover the truth.

Even so, an attitude of openness to ideas and experiences is only good up to a point. A child may encounter a household situation that warrants parental words of clarity and caution. Some situations may be too much for young children to understand. Parents need to be prepared to help guide their children if they face modern situations that are confusing when compared with their own family life. This principle applies to other areas as well. A faith-filled college student, for example, does well to dialogue with his friend who does not believe in God, and try to better understand his perspective. This does not mean, however, that he should immerse himself in the writings of Friedrich Nietzsche on the recommendation of his atheist friend.

DATING

During adolescence healthy dating involves planned group activities with both young men and women such as ice skating, a church-sponsored service or social event, a school-sponsored dance with a high human tone, or a gathering in a home for board games or other such activities while parents are also present. An intimate and intense personal relationship between a young man and a young woman is not wise until both are older. Premature intimacy in relationship can monopolize one's time and interior resources, limiting opportunities for wholesome growth. And then there are the complications associated with a relationship that is by nature ordered toward discerning a vocation to marriage. Young hearts grow ever fonder of the other, at times passionately longing for the fulfillment that the other seems to bring. When hearts become so engaged, only two possibilities remain: a break-up, which will most likely be difficult, or an eventual marriage.

Parents do well to point this out to their children. They should also point out that another person, even in marriage, can never provide complete fulfillment. It is wrong for someone to burden another person with this task. The longings of the human heart are truly longings for God. Only God can provide the ultimate fulfillment we desire. This means that personal dating makes most sense when someone is ready to enter marriage in the near future.

ADDICTIONS

The human heart is drawn toward the good things of this world. It is heroic for a person to live the virtue of temperance to the point where he or she is able to properly enjoy legitimate pleasures while being detached from them, knowing that they are merely pointing toward a fulfillment that cannot happen in this world. Examples of intemperance in our times abound. Small children crave sugar and can easily indulge these cravings to excess. Young and old alike find modern forms of entertainment, like videos and electronic games, quite enticing. Some will binge watch a show or spend excessive amounts of time playing video games. The natural human desire to know about the world and others, to be social, has met a powerful medium in the online world. Many young people and adults are intemperate in the information they consume online, through social media or "news" websites. In the face of these enticements, we all need to struggle to live temperance. Repeated intemperate behavior can lead to addictive patterns that if not checked could become deep-seated. Even so, true addictions often have other causes along with just intemperance. Perhaps someone is drawn to seek satisfaction in the first place to cover up an inner wound resulting from harmful experiences. It is often the combination of factors that leads to serious addictions.

Whatever the cause, it can be difficult for someone on his or her own to overcome addictions; help from others is necessary. Parents certainly have a role to play if their child struggles with an addiction. There is a place for the decisive exercise of parental authority to remove problematic substances or content, or to stop certain behaviors, whatever the addiction entails. Wise parents will combine their exercise of authority with understanding and compassion. They will not be surprised if their child rebels under what he or she sees as an imposition, as the removal of freedom. They know that the heart rebels against the absence of what it deeply desires. Parents may calmly explain that, rather than taking away their child's freedom, the decisive steps taken are actually intended to help foster authentic freedom, not that they expect that their child will express acceptance of this explanation. Perhaps the most difficult thing about such situations is the parental strength required to continue to exercise loving authority when their child does everything in his or her power to make it seem that such authority is unjust.

Wise parents also know that, in addition to forcibly tearing an addiction from the heart, it is necessary to help a wounded heart find whatever healing it needs. If there is a wound that caused the young heart to originally seek out addictive behavior then this wound will likely still be there. Help may be needed to find inner healing and peace. Likewise, breaking the hold of an addiction on the heart will be made much easier if the heart is presented with other goods to which it can attach in the right way. Part of the process of healing could involve finding concrete ways to serve others, to forget about oneself and give generously to others.

And while parents should have confidence in their authority and good judgment there is definitely a role for seeking advice and support. We can all benefit from talking through difficult family situations with someone we trust who has the necessary experience and perspective. With some types of addictions, it may be helpful to seek out someone with professional expertise.

CHAPTER 5

Witnessing to the Truth

Parents do well to instruct their children in the truth about God's plan for the attractions of the human heart, marital love, and the family. If parents and other educators do this properly, a child will see human love in the context of a lived supernatural outlook, an active sense of the transcendent battle between good and evil that is taking place around us, and the role of each of us as a child of God. Instruction comes not only from what parents say, but from what they do. Our actions indicate commitment to God's plan.

Parents know that their own actions need to be consistent with what they tell their children. Any inconsistency will be, at the very least, confusing. A father who talks about modesty but then proceeds to walk around the house half-dressed sends a mixed message to his children. This becomes more complicated when we think about children observing parental responses to the actions of other people. A girl who hears her mother's explanation that marriage is a great sacrament uniting one man to one woman will watch very closely how she talks to a relative involved in a same-sex relationship. The child will be looking to see how her mother balances kindness with truthfulness.

Most people today readily understand the need for kindness, even if being kind is understood in a somewhat simplistic way, as merely "accepting" the other. People nowadays hear about the need to avoid being judgmental.[1] Tolerance is seen as important. And it is true that we do need to accompany others in their search to do what is right through a genuine offer of friendship. If we avoided anyone who was not living according to the commandments of God, we would be failing in a fundamental way in our obligation to try to help others discover the healing love of God.

---

1. The way people use the word "judgmental" today is open to equivocation. Nearly everyone agrees that making rash judgments is wrong, that assuming the worst about someone without adequately knowing the situation is a fault. On the other hand, most people will admit that it is important to follow the judgments of conscience, that there is a serious problem with someone who does what he believes to be wrong in a particular situation. But the way the word "judgmental" is often used fails to make an adequate distinction between our duty to form judgments about the right thing to do and the failure to do this through being rash, instead subtly implying that legitimate and necessary judgments are suspect.

In balancing kindness with a commitment to the truth we need to make a distinction between an action that communicates one's personal agreement with error and an action to assist a person who suffered a moral lapse. Authentic charity is never consistent with the former, although it can be consistent with the latter. It is wrong to give public witness to a ceremony considered illicit by the Church. On the other hand, offering material support and friendship to an unwed mother who carries her baby to term is not supporting sexual relations between unmarried people. The act of assisting the young woman in need does not imply approval of the action which led to that need.

A PARENT'S DILEMMA

But what about parents who are faced with deciding whether to attend the "marriage" ceremony of their child, when they believe a true marriage is not taking place? Many well-intentioned people have arrived at different answers as to what a parent should do.

Some parents, after carefully considering the circumstances and the nature of the relationships involved, judge that the best thing is to attend the ceremony. For such a decision to be legitimate, it is important that everything necessary for a natural marriage is present, including a man and a woman, without any obvious impediments to marriage, intending to enter into a life-long commitment that includes an openness to forming a family. If these basic conditions are met and the parents have explained to all close people, including their child, that their attendance is not meant to witness or celebrate the union but rather express a commitment to helping to straighten things out for the couple in the future, then it may be best for one or both of the parents to attend. To do this, parents would need to judge that non-attendance would damage the parent-child relationship to such an extent that future assistance to help regularize the marriage would be highly unlikely.

Other parents may judge that the risks of attending such a ceremony are not worth it. They reason that almost no matter what a parent says or does, his or her actions will be interpreted as condoning an invalid marriage. They note that by being present and witnessing to a solemn ceremony, such as one intended to unite persons in marriage, the common assumption is that we are affirming with our presence our approval and agreement with what is happening.

Their concern is not only with what people in general may think but also with the message given to their child. At some point in the future the child's conscience may begin to awaken, causing doubt as to whether it was good to enter such a union. This doubt is a good thing and can even be the result of the movements of God's grace. The first step in a conversion is coming to realize where they have gone wrong, where they need to change. If the child remembers back and thinks of his or her parents witnessing the union, it may be more difficult for the child to acknowledge the wrong. On the other hand, parents who respectfully decline the invitation to the ceremony send a strong message to their child, a message that can, over time, help to lead to a conversion, although in the short term it may cause pain.

AVOIDING SCANDAL

Traditionally, the requirement to fully witness to the truth in such situations has been called our moral obligation to avoid causing scandal. We do wrong when our actions lead others to error or wrongdoing. Our Lord was very clear on this, noting that death by drowning would be preferable to leading one of his little ones to sin (see Lk 17:2). Though not popular, this traditional teaching is fundamentally sound and cannot change since it is rooted in the obligation we have to our brothers and sisters to witness to the truth. When, by our actions, we take a stand for what is right, we not only witness to those close to us, but also make a positive contribution to the overall moral tone of society. Uncommon or difficult ethical stands rarely go unnoticed. We can help undo the overall lukewarm attitude of moral compromise that has resulted, in no small part, from people failing to adequately consider the common good in an expansive way.

The notion of a transcendent moral order demanding certain actions and forbidding others makes perfect sense to a child. Just as part of the oddness of fairyland is that striking a certain bell dooms a city to destruction, so it is fitting that telling a lie to someone is not insignificant, that our obligation to speak truthfully is based in a real and objective moral order. Living according to this moral order is serious business and will be known as such by those raised under the "Ethics of Elfland," to use G. K. Chesterton's phrase from his book

Orthodoxy. This respect for the moral order and for the truth is what adults are also called to preserve. It is sad when someone grows old in an unhealthy way, in a way that teaches him to compromise these fundamental commitments.

THE HOME

The implications of our obligation to witness to the truth in our actions goes beyond attending or not attending certain ceremonies. Much is communicated by social interactions as well. When we invite someone into our home, to join in a meal with our family, this is conveying a sense of welcome and concord. The home is a place where it is natural to be "at home," to be able to comfortably lower our guard, knowing that all is fundamentally in a proper order. The outside world is good, as created by God and under his providence. But it is a place of struggle as well, an arena where the children of God act with the wisdom of serpents and the simplicity of doves (see Mt 10:16), each playing a small role in the drama of the great victory that he has already won. Human meetings and interactions that take place in the public sphere can be more formal and reserved.

A meeting in your home implies comfort and intimacy. It conveys that this person is someone who can be trusted to communicate with your children. A person welcomed into your home does not necessarily have to be in full agreement with all your values and convictions. But it may not be ideal to extend a welcome to your family dinner table to someone for whom there is an obvious impediment to embracing and living the truth. It might be better to meet such an acquaintance or relation in a neutral public place. It may be acceptable to extend a limited welcome into your home to such a person, even your own child, but only after a careful and prudent discernment. If you have younger children still living at home, it is important to think carefully about what messages your actions communicate to them.

THE HEART OF THE FATHER

On the other hand, this caution and distance can be taken too far. Your younger children should never get the sense that their older sibling is no longer a part of the family. Even when setting up clear boundaries, you should actively seek opportunities to continue to foster a relationship. Plan a picnic gathering for family and friends at a nearby part, warmly welcoming those for whom a visit in your home may be a bit awkward. Excellent food and upbeat games can help to make such a gathering enjoyable and formative for all involved. Host a private dinner at a restaurant for your son and his fiancée to show them that you want to continue to have a close relationship with them even though you judge it best not to attend the upcoming "marriage" ceremony.

The father in the parable of the Prodigal Son eagerly waits for the return of his son (see Lk 15:11–32). When the son is still far off, the father runs to him, covers him with a new robe, and gives him sandals and a ring. Likewise, children who separate themselves from the family home need to be made ready, to be properly adorned, before returning. But this making ready, this adornment, is very much the work of welcoming parents, actively looking for the return of their child, as well as the work of the child who starts the journey home. Parents of a child living a life estranged from the truth who are not actively seeking their child like the father in the parable, who scans the horizon for any sign of his son's return, run the risk of being too much like the older son: at home in a superficial sense but yet distant from, and perhaps even an impediment to, God's mercy. They may even cause scandal in a different way, sending a message to others, including their children, that religious practice is bound up in family strife. A cold commitment to truth without the warmth of an active charity that seeks out a relationship could, for example, push a teenage daughter to reject the faith which seems potentially divisive to the family she hopes to form someday.

The tension between an uncompromising commitment to the truth, with all its demands, and an unwavering commitment to an active charity is difficult to live. It is easy to say that there can be no authentic charity without truth and that a commitment to the truth demands charity as well. It is not surprising that many seek ways to lessen the cross of this tension, usually by thinking that it is acceptable to opt for charity over truth.

People of strong convictions today often think it is necessary, for the sake of family unity, to extend an unlimited welcome to relatives who are in irregular relationships. They use the same justification to attend ceremonies intended to join people in irregular arrangements. But many who are in such relationships do not really want to experience the cauterizing fire of true charity, the charity that loves someone into a right relationship with God. Rather, they want acceptance of their irregular situation.

It is true that your commitment to the truth may alienate the one you love, even your child, your spouse, or your other children. But it is also possible that if you couple your commitment to the truth with charity, your witness may help the other return to a right relationship with God and reality. If it is necessary or prudent for a parent to avoid being with a wayward child in a particular situation, it is all the more necessary for the parent to actively engage his or her child, seeking venues where a cordial and warm relationship can flourish. In any case, a parent should derive no small amount of comfort from the fact that our obligation is to be faithful to the correct path, even if it means that in the short-term things may appear worse. We do well to seek guidance from a wise person, to reflect deeply, and to pray earnestly. Then we can be at peace knowing that what is expected of us is faithfulness, not success. And through our faithfulness to prayer, we trust that God will bring about success in the end.

CHAPTER 6

Forming the Moral Imagination through Story

THE IMPORTANCE OF STORIES

Children can learn a great deal from the words and example of their parents and others. There is also a role for specific moral and religious instruction. But a commitment to living the truth in charity is best fostered when these means are complemented by rich examples present in good literature.

Good teachers know that students learn best when the teacher first reminds them of what they already know and then shows how new knowledge builds upon this foundation. A teacher intending to explain the classical roots of the thought behind the United States Constitution, for example, could first remind the class about the historical context of the document, taking a narrative approach that includes stories about the key founding fathers. A discussion of the challenges of becoming educated in colonial times could provide a natural segue into examining the Roman source texts for the founders' political thought.

Students learn better and find learning more enjoyable when the teacher employs a narrative context to help them make sense of what is being taught. Just as human thought begins when the mind forms a mental image from what the senses perceive and then abstracts an idea or concept from that image, so genuine learning involves engaging the imagination in a way that leads to the consideration of patterns and connections. And so a person is led from considering simple material details to the contemplation of profound truths. From the image of a merchant in search of fine pearls selling everything for the Pearl of Great Price, we consider how it makes sense to give up everything for the kingdom of God (see Mt 13:45–46).

While even adults learn best when a teacher employs a narrative method, this is particularly true for children. Children are less able to reason abstractly than adults. It takes a while for people to build up their rational prowess, a process aided by the study of mathematics and formal logic. Young children are not ready for the study of philosophy. The abstract science of metaphysics, which is rightly called wisdom, is beyond their capacity. But even young children have some use of reason and the ability to grasp profound truths when they are presented in the context of a story.

The traditional designation of seven as the age when reason typically awakens should not be rigidly understood. When one of our boys was three years old he was caught by an older brother rummaging through the bedroom searching for candy. When scolded, the younger replied, "But I haven't reached the age of reason yet!"

Young children can grasp profound truths when they are presented in a narrative form. They come to see that the world is fundamentally good as created by God. They understand that evil has come into the world through sin, that God has a plan to deal with evil, and that he is ultimately in charge of all of history. Children learn that their role is to rely on Father God and that their prayers and actions, when offered to God, do make a difference. Therefore, well-chosen children's literature and the stories of good teachers convey profound truths that help to form children's moral imagination so that they understand reality correctly, with hearts open to transcendence and love.

LITERATURE AND HUMAN LOVE

As children grow older, good literature and the right stories can play an important role in helping them to deeply understand God's plan for the love between a man and a woman, marriage, and the family. Years ago these stories reinforced a vision of masculinity and femininity that was also supported by the culture in general. Today the culture is sending mixed messages.

It may be worthwhile to note the source of the confusion here. There is something different going on today. People who have been educated according to the modern progressive system are trained that objective knowledge only comes from the methods of the empirical sciences. This self-imposed limitation of the scope of human reason results in a divided view of reality. On the one hand is the outside world, understood as a conglomeration of passive construction units arranged in various functional combinations, and on the other hand is the interior world of the human psyche, a world dominated by emotions.

One of the casualties of this paradigm is the notion that there is such a thing as a natural order in general and human nature in particular, a stable reality grounding all of us in a common humanity. We no longer understand what nature means and thus it is not surprising that we are losing the ability to ponder what it means to be human. Without this stable grounding, we find it difficult to know how to live our lives and structure our society. If we are honest, we will note that all of us suffer from this mindset and that it is a constant battle to gain perspective.

Thankfully, many people today would agree that we need to be discerning in evaluating historical or literary images of masculinity and femininity to determine what represents patterns of oppression and what reveals something authentic. However, the more fundamental point is that we need to be convinced that there is a meaning to our being human—as embodied persons male and female. The alternative is that there is no human nature and that *what we are* is subject to unlimited technological domination and manipulation.

We need to be clear about what the word "oppression" refers to. Is it evil, a perversion of good through sin, that is oppressive; or is it the notion of human nature itself that is oppressive? Recognizing that part of our problem today is a rejection of nature itself, of a natural created order, and that we are all implicated in this mindset, helps us gain perspective. It enables us to become explorers, searching for ancient wisdom, a partly obscured vision of what it means to be human. We are ready to begin the adventure of discovering truths about our being created male and female in well-chosen literature from the past.

For this reason, with the mindset of explorers searching for treasure, we turn to literature in search of images of what it means to be embodied creatures created male and female. What follows are images of wholesome human love and authentic masculinity and femininity from a few works of literature. No image is a perfect representation of such realities as the full meaning of human love and relationality. But well-chosen images can provide more than a glimpse of human nature. These images can provide an ideal, a model to which we strive to conform our behavior.

THE LITTLE BRITCHES SERIES BY RALPH MOODY

This eight-book autobiographical series tells the tale of a family through the eyes of Ralph, the second of six children. The tale begins in 1906 when eight-year-old Ralph and his family move from New Hampshire to Colorado to become ranchers. The family encounters and overcomes hardships, including the death of Ralph's father when the children are still young. Ralph's father is an image of calm and determined leadership. He earns the respect of other ranchers by thinking through a plan to fairly distribute the scarce water from a stream. He treats young Ralph as his little partner in the ranching and homesteading adventure and has some tender and fatherly conversations with him when Ralph gets into trouble through boyish imprudence. He uses the image of building character through actions and, rather than harshly punishing wrongdoing, leads his son to a deep love and repentance.

Ralph's mother presents a truly amazing image of feminine courage and strength. She continually attempts to raise the cultural tone in the home, reading literature to the family in the evenings and insisting that her children dress well when going out in public or to school. Ralph is mercilessly persecuted for a time by classmates who see him as trying to be a little gentleman. After her husband's death Ralph's mother holds the family together and finds ways for the older children to help the family earn enough to survive. She searches for and obtains work caring for linens and fine garments. And when she realizes that she is going to be forced to give testimony that, though true, would probably end up unjustly incriminating a man, she presents the problem to her older children. Through her leadership, the problem is presented as fundamentally a moral one, and only secondarily as a practical one, and the response of her older children is in full agreement with her assessment of the situation. They end up fleeing Colorado and heading back east to avoid the injustice. And through all the hardships that the family faces she remains faithful to the memory of her late husband, making sure the children never experience the complete absence of the father they lost.

THE LORD OF THE RINGS
BY J. R. R. TOLKIEN

Tolkien wrote *The Silmarillion*, *The Hobbit*, and *The Lord of the Rings* trilogy not simply to present a wonder-filled fantasy world.[1] He wrote these works for the education and formation of his children, specifically to try to remind them of an older and more noble way of viewing reality than the reductive modern outlook. Tolkien was concerned that the modern mindset was making it difficult for people to correctly see reality. The world of Middle Earth was his way to help us see the world in which we live in a more complete way.

We exist in a moral universe where there is a real battle raging between good and evil and in this context human actions have transcendent meaning. Hobbits may be simple folk who lack the power

---

1. If you have not read these books yet, I recommend starting with *The Hobbit* and then reading *The Lord of the Rings*. Save *The Silmarillion* for last.

of great warriors, elven lords, or wizards, but their contribution is important and can even be decisive. Providence, never spoken about directly, is assumed throughout the work and the wise remain true to the right path by recognizing that there are deeper purposes at work even in the darkest moments. Tolkien's inoculation against the perils of reductionism is best complemented for older children by learning sound philosophy. But I would argue that to attempt to counter reductionism or scientism through teaching sound philosophy alone will be much less effective. A two-pronged approach— reaching the moral imagination as Tolkien does and teaching sound philosophy—is necessary to address the problem that Tolkien saw so clearly: we are all already strongly influenced by materialist philosophies.

Tolkien's work is like a keen-edged sword drawn and masterfully taking the offensive against the reductionism that surrounds us. He succeeds in restoring a transcendent outlook, including a proper sense of nature and an openness to the supernatural. In this context, he presents powerful images of masculinity, femininity, and human love. Authentic masculinity is revealed through the characters of Aragorn and Faramir. In Aragorn we see the humble king in exile who knows that true royal power is for the good of his people. His strength is tempered by prudence and perspective and he leads through service. The family of the stewards of Gondor is more complicated. Denethor and Boromir both meet tragic ends, the former by pride and despair, and the latter by pride and a disordered desire for the power to prevail in a way not tempered by wisdom. Boromir repents and dies a noble death in the end. Faramir, however, like Aragorn is a true leader and servant of the good. He refuses the power Boromir sought and strives to do his duty in the face of what appears to be overwhelming odds.

Tolkien also presents tremendous images of feminine strength in such figures as Galadriel and Eowyn of Rohan. While others head off to battle, Galadriel uses her power to protect the enchanted wood of Lothlorien and is engaged in a continuous interior battle with the dark one whom she knows is more powerful than her. Others see the peaceful, restorative fruit of her tremendous interior struggles. She knows the power of the evil one and yet perseveres along the path of hope, rejecting the power of the ring when it is offered to her. Without the slightest hint of the tendency in contemporary feminism to rebel against the feminine, to rebel against nature, Tolkien presents Eowyn as a maiden warrior who, with the help of a hobbit, defeats a terror no living knight could match in battle. Like Galadriel, Eowyn is acting according to a deeper calling to be a steward of humanity and we can take her to be an image of feminine strength reminiscent of some extraordinary European women in the medieval period.

A word of caution on the Lord of the Rings movies: In general these movies do a better job showing the evil in Middle Earth than the good. The movies are not faithful to the books in several key ways. The entire character of Faramir is misrepresented. Modern romantic themes are imported into Tolkien's work by some liberty with the character of Arwen. The movies generally do not do a great job at portraying the women characters of Tolkien's novels. The books are much better and someone would do well to not allow the rich images that Tolkien's narrative presents to be compromised by the overlay of images attained from watching the movies.

DAVID COPPERFIELD
BY CHARLES DICKENS

Throughout his novels, Dickens excels in presenting characters of diverse types and personalities. He writes with a strong sense of compassion for those who suffer unjustly at the hands of others and especially those whose misery comes from unjust societal structures. Like many of Dickens' novels, *David Copperfield* is long. But the reader will be well rewarded by, among other things, getting to know Agnes Wickfield, the image of a perfect Victorian woman whose virtues transcend her cultural context. She is kind, intelligent, loving, patient, sympathetic, merciful, strong-willed, discreet, and faithful. Dickens masterfully presents marriage, including the marriage of David and Agnes, with all its relational complexities and possibilities, including keen insights about how men and women complement each other.

OTHER HELPFUL LITERATURE

Jane Austen's novels—especially *Pride and Prejudice*, *Sense and Sensibility*, *Emma*, and *Mansfield Park*, where character matters most—are excellent literature and helpful in understanding perennial truths about men and women and their relationships. Jane Austen is not just for girls, although they may be developmentally ready to read her work earlier than boys. Older boys can benefit tremendously from her writings. There is likewise much wisdom in many of Shakespeare's plays. *The Merry Wives of Windsor*, for example, humorously presents the vices of an unguarded heart in the character of Sir John Falstaff and the virtuous response of the sensible Mistresses Ford and Paige. *Sir Gawain and the Green Knight* explores the tension in relationships between men and women and how this tension relates to the need for a well-guarded heart.

The *Kristin Lavransdatter* trilogy by Sigrid Undset, while a bit too dark for some, does an excellent job of presenting the implications of imprudent decisions made by young hearts as well as the possibility of redemption. The great Russian novelists Dostoyevsky, Tolstoy (his early works, especially *Anna Karenina*—avoid his later works like *Resurrection*) and Turgenev (his *Fathers and Sons*) all have quite a bit in them. *The Betrothed* by Alessandro Manzoni is a real gem.

George MacDonald is also an interesting author. His fairy tales were very influential for C. S. Lewis and J. R. R. Tolkien. Lewis described reading him as a "baptism" of the imagination. MacDonald presents rich images of masculinity and femininity.

SCRIPTURE

Within Scripture, stories powerfully convey truths about men and women and human love. Parents can read to their children such passages as the story of the marriage of Isaac and Rebecca from the Book of Genesis. Rebecca accepts the invitation to marry Isaac as a vocational call. When Abraham's servant arrives and explains his prayer and errand, she perceives the call of God in the invitation to leave her home and family in order to begin a new life with Isaac in a distant land. Her uncle notes that the calling is from the Lord, not something for him to question or challenge.

In contrast to the popular and deficient understanding of freedom as keeping open as many options as possible, Rebecca uses her freedom for choosing the path God sets before her. We see that a vocation involves using freedom for a purpose, for making a commitment.

The entire Book of Tobit is an engaging story of faithfulness to God's plan, even when faced with great hardships and suffering. The marriage of Tobias and Sarah is a union that is entered into with humility and trust in God's providential plan. Tobias and Sarah receive each other on their wedding night as two children of the promise who seek above all to honor God through their union. The broader communal dimensions of a marriage are present in both stories of Rebecca and Tobit, an appealing side of marriage that is not emphasized as much in our highly mobile and urban society.

CHAPTER 7

Technology in the Governance of Our Homes

The proliferation of television and other screens has led to changes in how a typical family spends time at home. Today children and adults spend a significant amount of time at home interacting with screen content or with others in a way mediated through screens. Some such interactions are quick, like glances at a cell phone, and others are more prolonged, such as watching movies or keeping up with relatives and friends through social media. In the past, instead of such screen time, family members spent more time interacting directly with each other, working, writing letters to distant relatives or friends, and reading books.

Computers and screens, if used well, can enrich family life. A family movie night, where a well-chosen film is enjoyed together, can be a source of family unity and have educational value, including forming the moral imagination of children. Computers can be used well for communication: video conferencing with distant relatives and friends, or organizing meal help for a family who has a sick child. And computers provide the possibility of easily connecting with information and cultural material that would astound our ancestors.

In many homes, however, these positive benefits of computers are mixed with negatives as well. In some families, excessive screen time reduces wholesome human contact. And not all uses of screens are enriching. Time wasted on mindless content and gaming is, unfortunately, common. And some content is problematic and deformative: Websites glorify violence, promote dangerous ideologies, and present pornography. There are algorithms that make addiction more likely. There is a danger of echo chamber information due to search engine algorithms. And sorting through the accuracy of information is not easy for young people on the internet.

Faced with these problems, some families eliminate, or greatly reduce, the number of screens in their homes. Given the real dangers that some online content poses to children and teenagers, the decision to eliminate or mostly eliminate screens is not unreasonable. Nonetheless, children need to learn how to live in a world in which screens are increasingly present, in public, and in the workplace.

The following points about governance of the home help strike the right balance:

SCREEN USE FROM A VIRTUE PERSPECTIVE

It is very easy to waste time using screens. Video games, social media, and the nearly endless flow of information and entertainment that screens can provide are all problematic apart from any intrinsically immoral content.

Time is a treasure that is meant to be used well, to be sanctified. We are blessed to live in an affluent era when most of us have free time that we can determine how to use after completing necessary work. Instead of using their freedom to pursue some good—diligent study of something, learning a foreign language, fostering a meaningful hobby, service work, or even time spent caring for family members—many seek to simply pass the time. Not having made a conscious decision to use time well, they fall into a dissipated and passive mode of wanting to be entertained. At best this leads to a potentially harmful curiosity, and at worst to a dull boredom that borders on despair.

DANGERS OF PORNOGRAPHIC CONTENT

Though it is good for parents to be concerned about the potential for time-wasting that screens present, wasting time is not the only problem. Screens are used extensively today for viewing pornography. Many people, both men and women, are addicted to pornographic content. Most of these people never intended for this to happen. Many were drawn in by readily available content and clever selling techniques. Teenagers are particularly vulnerable, as they are often inquisitive and impulsive, lacking the sound judgment characteristic of adulthood.

PUBLIC PLACES ONLY

People in leadership positions often make decisions informed by considering potential risks. Risk management is an important part of strategic business decision making. Allowing children to connect to the online world in the apparent privacy of their bedrooms is a risk that is best avoided. Children should not be expected to square off alone in a private battle with an online world in which powerful forces vie for their attention, forces seeking to profit from their continued engagement. Tech companies employ attention engineers to design platforms that promote frequent and prolonged use, a key factor in profitability. These strategies are not foreign to the highly profitable pornography industry. For this reason all devices capable of connecting to the Internet should typically be in public places surrounded by lots of family traffic.

SMART PHONES

The very term "smart phone" is an outdated misnomer. Smart phones are small computers with significant capabilities. The time spent talking on these devices as phones is significantly less than the time spent using them for other purposes. As with other screens and portable devices, it is risky for parents to burden their children with the responsibility of using these devices properly. Wise parents employ various means to "dumb down" these phones, such as disabling the browser and only allowing certain applications.

Many adults also struggle with using their smart phones properly. The benefits of these devices do not always outweigh the downsides, even if only time wasted on trivial content. It is possible even for adults to live with a "dumbed down" phone. A strong character, including the virtues of prudence and temperance, is necessary to use smart phones without allowing them to become a source of undue distraction. It is truly extraordinary for an older teen to have such a strong character.

USING FAMILY COMPUTERS WELL

Sensible parents will put procedures in place to help promote temperate uses of computers. While exact details vary from family to family, most parents will set limits as to when computers can be used and when they should be turned off, such as a specified shut-down time in the evening. Some parents require children to ask permission prior to any use of computers. They expect children to state what they intend to do on the computer and then ask for permission to use it. Use for entertainment is best done as a planned social activity. While it can be enjoyable to watch wholesome videos as a group in a planned way, it is not healthy for people to fill down time with screen use.

EMAIL AND SOCIAL MEDIA NORMS

Computers are powerful communication and information accessing tools. The challenge is to benefit from these capabilities without wasting time as a consumer of entertainment or exposing ourselves to harmful content. Not all uses of email and other social media platforms are equally helpful.

Parents should be discerning in what social media they allow their children to use. It is best to spend time with children beginning to use social media to help explain positive and negative uses. Children need to know that everything they do online is publicly available. Many later regret their youthful social media posts, which can and have resulted in college acceptances being rescinded and even difficulties getting or keeping a job.

CHAPTER 8

Adults and the Virtue of Holy Purity

It would be a mistake to assume that we need to be perfect before being able to credibly talk to others about pure and noble human love. If this were true, then no parent would ever be up to the task of parenting. Fortunately, children do not expect nor need perfection from their parents. Children are actually fairly tolerant of faults in others and, in their simple way, are edified when they see efforts being made to do the right thing when it is difficult. They tend not to be judgmental, rather taking at face value the notion that a continuous struggle to do what is right is part of the human condition, even for adults.

Even so, children do learn from the example of their parents. They are continually comparing what they are told by their parents with the way their parents live their lives. They have a strong sense for hypocrisy. They may not expect perfection but will be unimpressed with the explanation of an ideal that has no bearing on the way the speaker lives. Children may not have direct knowledge of their parent's interior moral life, but they will know if the way you talk to them and show affection is consistent with someone who is struggling to love with refinement. This is so much the case that the best lesson in pure love that you can give your children is your own efforts to live the virtue of holy purity.

THE HUMAN HEART

Every honest person knows that the human heart is capable of, and even drawn toward, sin and that each person must at times struggle against desires that should not be fulfilled. As our Lord warns, what comes from the outside is not as big of a problem as that which comes from within. "For out of the heart come evil thoughts, murder, adultery, fornication, theft, false witness, slander" (Mt 15:19). The sources of sin that tend to move our hearts are aptly described as the seven capital sins: pride, covetousness, lust, anger, gluttony, envy, and sloth. Initial movements of the heart described by these capital sins are not necessarily themselves sinful: The person experiences these movements as a given and then has to decide how to act. Sin is not present until there is an act of the will.

It is not uncommon for external situations to trigger inner tendencies toward sin. For example, a man struggling to make ends meet experiences envy as a sadness at the good fortune of a neighbor with an abundance of wealth. He can react in different ways: negatively, by seeking illicitly what he could not gain by honest means, or positively, by giving thanks for his many blessings, not the least among them the blessing of knowing poverty. Likewise, someone's initial anger when cut off in traffic, itself not chosen, gives way to charity when a prayer is said for the offending driver.

LIVING HOLY PURITY

In one sense the challenges associated with living holy purity fall within this broader paradigm: The heart's attraction toward another person or image is rejected as the person interiorly turns in another direction, perhaps toward our Lady or St. Joseph.

This is easier said than done. The sheer volume of problematic images a person typically encounters in a normal day is a challenge. Images on screens and images in print are prevalent in the public spaces in which we live. In a typical supermarket, on electronic billboards, and online advertising, we see a reductive view of the human person as attractive flesh and bone, and nothing more.

SEEING AND LOOKING

But while it may not be possible to avoid *seeing* problematic images, it is possible to avoid *looking* at them, by redirecting your focus to other things. Granted, looking away is not easy when faced with a constant barrage of images. You do well not to become scrupulous, worrying if a glance at the advertisement on the side of the screen was born out of impure curiosity or not. Have the humility to view the adventure of guarding the eyes as a game of sorts, a positive effort to focus your own attention rather than be distracted by those vying to present their product or agenda.

If someone ends up taking that second look, or gives something impure more consideration than it deserves, it is common—and this could be the result of a trick of the devil—to right away feel compromised, even to the point of wondering if all is lost. This thought can lead to a further introspective dialogue that is, at the very least, not helpful. As soon as you notice such an interior dialogue, cut it off decisively. Say an act of contrition and perhaps resolve to mention this struggle in your next confession and then stop thinking about it. Sometimes interior peace is best restored by removing yourself from the situation and becoming occupied with something else. The basic ascetical point is that the brave thing to do in the face of temptations against purity is to flee. A dialogue with the temptation does not go well. Any attempt to directly face such a temptation will almost necessarily involve some type of compromise of interior integrity.

It helps to see the struggle for pure love as a defense of the interior fortress of your heart, where the prudent strategy is to go out and meet the enemy far from the fortress,[1] in such details as guarding your eyes and guarding your heart. Guarding your eyes consists in the mortification of continually

---

1. See Josemaría Escrivá, *The Way*, 307.

looking away from not only problematic images but even at times from what is pleasant and wholesome to observe. Guarding your heart refers to a deeper disposition of fostering interior self-possession and integrity. A guarded heart is not easily distracted by the ephemeral but has built up a store of the fire of charity, a charity that loves God above all else and loves creatures rightly for his sake. This is important because of the pernicious way impure images can stay with a person, sticking to the heart. It is possible to check this content by guarding the interior senses of the imagination and exercising control over the desires of the heart.

CURIOSITY

To achieve this interior self-dominion it is necessary to fight against a vice that most people today do not realize is a vice: curiosity. That curiosity is a vice is a bit confusing to many. As an educator I have been asked to rate a student's curiosity as a measure of intellectual virtue on college recommendation forms. The author of this form is reflecting a general sense of curiosity as referring to the good of being intellectually engaged and interested in learning. Traditionally the virtue of studiousness is set in opposition to the vice of curiosity. Studiousness is the virtue by which someone focuses with a sustained spirit of study on mastering a particular body of knowledge. The vice of curiosity is opposed to real study in that the curious person is readily distracted. He gives in to abandoning the difficult intellectual work he should be doing in favor of learning about something tangential. The curious person moves from one thing to another without the order that is necessary to achieve comprehensive knowledge or mastery.

While intellectual discipline is still valued today, the reason curiosity is given such a positive spin is that we now face a much more serious intellectual problem. Today there is a growing sense of intellectual dullness, a boredom in the face of learning about anything. This is largely the result of the sensory overload of the modern entertainment industry and the prevalence of trivial information. People who surrender themselves to being captivated by an onslaught of images from a screen have a harder time experiencing reality at a human pace. People who frequently follow specific data trends or the latest on social media are all too easily caught up investing themselves in trivial matters, consciously sought distractions. Even though it may be true that dull boredom is a more serious problem than mere curiosity, just as despair is worse than naive optimism, it is still true that curiosity as dissipation is a vice.

Curiosity is also a vice that readily leads to problems in living the virtue of purity. When people are approaching a device that is able to access a rich store of information and images in a casual and non-focused way they are necessarily approaching it with a lowered guard. They are curious, wondering what information and images they will see, perhaps on social media or perhaps on some news website. This curious wondering easily slides into an unguarded openness to entertaining content. In this psychological state people are open to reading or seeing content that is odd, shocking, or even disturbing. Some of this content may be merely banal, like silly pictures or videos about overweight cats.

However, when people in such a psychological state encounter a sexual image or description, their weakened defenses buckle and collapse. The heart's openness, or even more so, the active seeking of the heart for the novel and entertaining, leads them to consume impure content that is perhaps, at first, both repulsive and attractive. It does not take long for content welcomed in this way to adhere to the heart, staying with them and returning through the imagination at often inopportune times, such as when they are tired or upset.

Living the virtue of holy purity today requires waging a vigorous ascetical battle against the vice of curiosity. This is key to keeping the battle for integrity of heart far away from the fortress of the heart. Practically this means the following:

APPROACH DEVICES AND INFORMATION WITH A PLAN

If curiosity is approaching content with a desire for entertainment, then we should never approach a device or text without a good purpose. For example, while it is good to be informed about world events and local news, it makes sense to seek this information in a deliberate and planned way. It is all too easy to approach catching up on news online as a way to indulge curiosity. Instead, people who plan to spend a set amount of time, perhaps seven minutes, accessing meaningful content will come away with a better understanding of the news without feeling the lethargy common after passively receiving content. Such people are actively engaging the device. For example, they first skim an article on an economic crisis from a popular news source, then go on to read an article from a more scholarly source. The set time elapses and they move on to another task. It can be an enjoyable adventure to see how much they can learn in a set amount of time.

This detail of exercising order through setting a time schedule for ourselves can go a long way to fostering a studious approach to information rather than a curious one. The same principle could help for keeping up on family and friends through social media. Approach the social media platform with a plan to spend only a specific amount of time and, perhaps, also the intention to say a short prayer for each friend or family member.

PLACE TIME LIMITS

Some people might argue that there is no place for watching videos of funny things pets do or other such content. It would be difficult to argue that such content is positively harmful. Much of it is simply wholesome fun. There is little wrong with a family sitting down and laughing together at such online content. The key is the virtue of order, exercised through a prudent planning of a set time for such family laughs. It is not necessarily indulging curiosity for a family to plan to watch fifteen minutes of funny videos after finishing chores. Sticking to the planned fifteen minutes can even be a way to help foster the virtue of temperance and order in children.

GROW IN STUDIOUSNESS

Avoiding a vice is only part of the battle; it is also necessary to grow in the corresponding virtue. In general it is not enough to progress merely by the negative path of denial. When something is removed from the heart, the empty spaces opened up are restless spaces. The heart continues to seek after something to which it can adhere.

It is more effective to focus on growth in virtue in addition to the removal of vice. Avoiding curiosity is avoiding a vice. Growing in studiousness is actively seeking a virtue that provides the interior strength most directly opposed to curiosity. Studiousness is a virtue that grows especially through setting aside time for focused study.

While it is difficult to add study as another task to an already overscheduled day, it is often quite possible to find room for study at work or at home by intentionally planning a schedule. This can lead to increased productivity, as Cal Newport argues convincingly in his book *Deep Work*.[2] People are becoming increasingly aware of the need to protect time for focused study and thinking. Productivity can be harmed, for example, by constant attention to email when at work. Studiousness is fostered by limiting time spent accessing online information and spending more time reading significant texts. It is helpful to come up with a reading plan that includes some material that requires sustained mental effort, such as a work of philosophy, as well as quality literature that can be enjoyed when tired. Spending some time

2. Cal Newport, *Deep Work: Rules for Focused Success in a Distracted World* (New York: Grand Central Publishing, 2016).

reading a good novel before going to bed can be a relaxing way to transition to sleep.

MORTIFICATIONS

What is a mortification? Mortifications are best thought of as prayers of the senses. A person denies himself some pleasure and calmly allows grace to transform this offering to an act of love of God. Prayer is any loving movement of the heart and mind to God. Experiencing a small sense of loss in an unfulfilled appetite can be lovingly added to the movement of our hearts toward God, becoming itself part of a prayer. Another way to say it is that mortifications can help bring our whole selves, including the senses, into a loving relationship with God. Mortifications aiming to restrict our attention to only certain things are best suited to countering the vice of curiosity. Examples include intentionally limiting what we choose to look at while walking down the street or not listening to the radio for a time while driving in the car. Not allowing our imagination to wander in fanciful directions can be a good mortification of the interior senses.

CHAPTER 9

Recovering from a Fall

It is all too easy for a wandering heart to find itself compromised by impure content. Most people who struggle in this area never intended to find themselves in trouble. Impure content sufficiently occupies our public spaces to make it challenging to maintain integrity of heart. And on top of that, there are many clever people who are exploiting the entertainment industry with harmful agendas, including profiting from those who become addicted to pornography. Every approach to an online platform brings the risk of a brush with morally questionable content.

And the way we tend to approach information is part of the problem. As mentioned earlier, curiosity is not generally understood as a vice, but rather as descriptive of a lively interest in learning. The initial giving in to curiosity in seeking interesting content leads to a general dissipated openness. In this state people easily take that second look at shocking or even repulsive impure content. Conscience awakens and they realize that there has been a fall, that integrity has been compromised. Then the thought presents itself that they are beyond redemption. The resolution to struggle weakens and they give in completely since "all is already lost." Even if they recover enough to continue the struggle, the memory of the fall remains, ready to surge to the surface at an inopportune time. This drama can play out to the point where people feel truly defeated and incapable of being friends of God. It can even reach the point where people are truly addicted to pornographic content, incapable by their own power to break free.

Recovery from a fall or a series of falls involves steps that break this cycle, steps that use both human means and rely on the help that God, as a loving Father, wants to send as well:

HUMILITY

You will know the truth, and the truth will make you free (Jn 8:32). Humility is fundamentally the recognition of the truth concerning who we are and who God is. Embracing the truth about our weakness and

God's strength helps us recover, even if the falls are many and come with addictive patterns. Simply put, the truth is that we carry great treasures—human freedom with all its possibilities and sanctifying grace, the very life of God himself—in weak vessels, hearts that have been wounded by sin and the complications this brings.

No matter how many times we fall God's desire for our turning back to him remains unchanged. Indeed, each fall is a chance to grow more deeply in a humility that recognizes that the tremendous gift God gives us, sharing in his own inner life, comes to those who look on the greatness of God more than on our weakness. God's strength is stronger than our weakness and it is manifested with clarity precisely in and through its ongoing transforming of human weakness.

CONFESSION

It is good devotional practice to pray an act of contrition, even several times each day. Many people are in the habit of doing an examination of conscience each evening followed by an act of contrition. After a fall one of the best things to do is express sorrow to

God and rely on his help to begin again. And it is the case that a perfect act of contrition, an act of a person moved by grace to have sorrow for sin primarily out of love for God as the one offended, is able to restore a person to a state of grace. We can make an act of contrition and begin again right after a fall. There is no need to give into a defeatist attitude! Even so, the normal way mortal sin is forgiven and sanctifying grace restored is through sacramental confession. And even someone who makes a perfect act of contrition will mention any sin which may have been mortal in his next confession as it is difficult to know if an act of contrition was perfect in the first place.

When going to confession it is not necessary or desirable to go into explicit details regarding sins of impurity. Mention simply and directly the type of sin and the approximate number of times it was committed. For example, people who are caught in addictive patterns in the beginning of the healing process may mention in confession the approximate number of times they intentionally looked at impure content. As God transforms them, they may fall in this way less frequently. The struggle will move more toward the vice of curiosity. In confession perhaps they mention wandering eyes looking at impure advertisements while reading legitimate informative content online, or wandering movements of the heart that are not checked right away.

Eventually someone may be so aware of the dangers of curious dissipation that he or she routinely reacts against such tendencies. They may confess faults such as filling some down time with looking at news websites rather than sticking to an intentional plan for learning about current world events. A careful examination of conscience may even reveal that there is some "background" curiosity open to impurity in such unguarded browsing of content. Someone who has brought the battle to the point where they are seeking God's help with such unguarded moments and the vice of curiosity could be well along the path to holiness.

ACCOUNTABILITY COACH

An additional person to talk with about the struggle on a practical level can be very helpful. Set up a regular time to meet with such a person to go over how the struggle is going. This person can help with setting specific resolutions. After talking through someone's history, for example, it might make sense to form a resolution of avoiding any online content at certain times of the day. Such practical strategizing is beyond what they should expect from the sacrament of confession.

ADDICTION COUNSELING

For some situations it is helpful or perhaps even necessary to seek help from someone with a particular expertise in the psychology of addictions. Certain addictive behaviors can establish patterns that make it difficult for someone to experience the transformative power of the sacrament of confession or be able to struggle for purity of heart.

For example, a person interiorly complicated by the compulsion that comes with addiction can easily fall into a scrupulous mental state that hinders openness to grace. A good confessor may recognize that the human means of a well-formed counselor with appropriate expertise could be just what is needed to help remove the human obstacles that are making it difficult for grace to be transformative.

OTHER HUMAN MEANS

Other helpful means to live purity include such things as filters for online content. An Internet filter is not a comprehensive solution and at best will be able to help keep an honest person honest. If you think placing significant trust in such a filter is wise just ask any tech savvy teenager how effective it really is.

It also may help to take up a hobby that helps spend downtime in a wholesome way. Such hobbies could include artistic endeavors such as painting or woodworking, cooking, taking walks, or even reading novels. Getting into the habit of using good manners when dealing with others can also help. Good manners can help elevate the tone and lead to an inner refinement that matches our outward actions.

DEVOTION TO OUR LADY

No consideration of the human heart could be complete without mentioning our greatest source of strength, the sure path to wholeness and victory. Devotion to Mary, perhaps under the title of Our Lady of Fair Love, is a tremendous help for those seeking to love with the warmth of purified human affections. It is for good reason that so many saints have recommended turning to Mary with matters of the heart. The heart of Mary, which knows no sin or disordered desires, fully identified with the mission of her son as he willingly poured out his life for us on the Cross. Mary, at the foot of the Cross, embraces her role as the new Eve, the mother of all the living, our Mother. Jesus not only entrusts St. John but also each of us to Mary with his words from the Cross, "Behold your son." Mary identifies with the full dimension of her vocation when she, who had no direct experience of sin, comes to know our sin by seeing its effects in her suffering son and yet fully embraces each of us sinners as her beloved child. Just as children trustingly flee to the warm arms of their mothers when injured or in danger, so we have only to flee to Mary's strong embrace. Her motherly care extends not only to helping clean what is soiled but also to training our hearts in the school of noble and fair human affections. With her help our hearts can love with refined passion and true charity.

CHAPTER 10

Encouragement

The birth of every child is an overwhelming testimony to God's fasithfulness to the world he has created and his total commitment to work his purposes in history. The coming into existence of a new human person is the result of so much more than a biological reproductive process. Unlike any other material thing, the form of each person is an immaterial and subsistent soul crafted individually by God.

Each human person is a unique masterpiece of God. None of the other living things we see in this world, even the most noble among the animals, are created in this way. One human person is worth more than the rest of material creation—including the vast expanses of space, the stars, and all lower forms of life—combined. But God's work of Creation pales compared to what he does to redeem us. As awesome as the creation of a human person is, the transformation of one soul through the sacrament of baptism is a greater work by far.

If God is so committed to the world he created and the human race he redeemed at such a great cost, how can we be pessimistic at the challenges facing parents today?

Sure, some things are different today. Sure, there are new challenges that we did not have to face growing up. We may not have had daily access to computers, let alone the Internet. We did not have the same bombardment of pressures from the media, pushing skewed agendas on a daily basis. Some of us remember a childhood that was much simpler and easygoing, with more imagination and play than the average child today. We rightly hope for the preservation of innocence in our children's hearts and minds, for each of our children to develop into their fullest potential without the onslaught of negative and damaging lies.

Practical parents know that there are no tasks to accomplish or clever parenting techniques which will guarantee success in the awesome task of raising children today. There are truths about God's plan for human love and the family that we need to pass on to our children, but the awesome task of parenting is so much more than conveying a curriculum.

The mission before us demands authenticity. Clever techniques cannot make up for failures to truly love God and others. These relationships have a fundamental priority over the strategies we employ. God must come first. Only a parent who is convinced that our dignity and value rest on the strongest of foundations, that we are loved by God, will be able to relate properly to others. And living as children of God transforms our relationships with others. It is the same heart, even if at times broken, that passionately loves those around us whom we see, and the God whom we do not see.

Raising children in our confused culture can seem like an overwhelming task. An honest parent readily recognizes that alone he or she is not up to this task.

But fortunately we are not alone.

God's commitment to us and our history is unshakeable. He is all in. He pours out his grace on those who pray and stay close to the sacraments. And there are many other parents who seek to live under God's mercy, to live as his children: imperfect parents, wounded and in need of healing grace, but manifesting the strength of God, at times precisely through human weakness.

Such parents are forming strong networks of faith-filled friends and families to share this journey. Strong friendships are forming. Children are experiencing authentic images of God's plan for human love and the family.

The foundations for a new culture of life are in place.